The best of the police log from the pages of the Lake Oswego Review newspaper

FIRST EDITION

A publication of the Lake Oswego Review
and the Pamplin Media Group
P.O. Box 548 | Lake Oswego, OR 97034

Publisher – J. Brian Monihan
Compiled by Lori Hall and Kara Hansen
Original police log written by Cliff Newell
Cover and book design by Dan Adams

FORWARD

When people find out that I work for the Lake Oswego Review, they always tell me the police blotter is their favorite part of the newspaper.

I couldn't agree more.

During a time when mainstream media is always reporting about impending doom and gloom, there

is something transcendent about reading the strange and sometimes goofy calls that local citizens make to the Lake Oswego Police Department.

After all, it's oddly comforting to live in a community where some of the biggest concerns revolve around where pets relieve themselves, why supposedly strange-looking people are walking through neighborhoods, whether ducks waddling in and out of traffic will make it across the road or what to do when kids act like zombies or play their music too loudly.

When these types of activities represent a significant portion of the calls to local police, it really does say a lot for the quality of life that Lake Oswego residents enjoy.

It also says a lot about the tremendous service the Lake Oswego Police Department provides. Officers' commitment to the idea that there is "no call too small" embodies the best of community policing, and we are grateful that Lake Oswego's finest embrace that motto and are always willing to serve and protect, no matter the level of call. Their dedication to serving Lake Oswego is something we all should never take for granted.

I also want to offer a special thanks to the reporters and editors who over the years have been tasked with compiling these blotter tidbits for each issue of the Lake Oswego Review. Cliff Newell has especially been instrumental in sifting through the call sheets to find these gems for us to share.

Thanks also to Lori Hall and Kara Hansen, who approached me with this idea more than a year ago. Because of their persistence and dedication, this book is in your hands today.

I hope you enjoy this collection of some of our favorite calls made to the Lake Oswego Police Department over the past five years. Hopefully your favorite blotter entries made it into the book as well.

J. Brian Monihan
Publisher – Lake Oswego Review

1/10/14 8:46 a.m. A turkey was going beserk running around in the street.

2009

1/4/09 12:06 a.m. Juveniles were plotting to steal Christmas decorations on Hastings Drive.

1/4/09 6:16 a.m. An employee arrived at work to find the phone off the hook and the door of the safe ajar on Boones Ferry Road. This turned out to be normal.

1/5/09 7:15 p.m. A car pulled over in front of a house, then turned into the driveway. It was last seen headed down Haven Street.

1/6/09 9:08 a.m. A man who found an injured squirrel placed it in a box, then called police.

1/6/09 4:03 p.m. Possibly threatening emails on Wood Thrush Street turned out to be a chain letter.

1/7/09 3:34 p.m. A homeowner who found the front door wide open called police, who blamed the suspicious incident on the wind.

1/7/09 4:03 p.m. Police located a 50-year-old man, who had left on a California trip the day before, and told him to call his mother.

1/7/09 4:12 p.m. A purse was inextricably marooned on the roof of a Fifth Street home.

1/11/09 10:11 a.m. A passerby expressed concern for several Boy Scouts. They were jumping in and out of a van to gather up Christmas trees on Amberwood Circle.

1/11/09 4:16 p.m. A plastic bag was spotted in the middle of Country Club Road.

1/12/09 8:48 a.m. A son who took a set of car keys from his mother refused to give them back.

1/13/09 10:20 a.m. Piles of white powder sprinkled on the paths at Springbrook Park turned out to be chalk marking the way for a cross country run.

1/14/09 11:59 a.m. A man was bothered via cellphone by a proficient and unwanted text messager.

1/14/09 3:15 p.m. A homeowner found two used matches and an open pack of cigarettes at the end of a driveway on Rainbow Drive. The next day they were gone.

1/15/09 10:37 a.m. Two apparent solicitors were walking up and down Lake Haven Drive carrying clipboards.

1/15/09 5:52 p.m. A lilac bush was the unfortunate victim of mischief on Suncreek Drive.

3/23/09 2:23 p.m. An elderly man in a white Buick seemed a bit disoriented at a stoplight on Country Club Road.

3/24/09 2:44 p.m. A customer who seemed jumpy at a bank completed their business and then left without causing any trouble.

3/24/09 7:32 p.m. A dog that constantly runs away from home has been using every yard in the neighborhood as a bathroom.

3/24/09 4:03 p.m. A daughter reported that her mother was driving like a maniac through town.

3/25/09 11:02 p.m. Suspicious males were seen sitting in a car two days in a row.

3/26/09 1:03 a.m. Two women thought to be burglarizing an apartment were actually "cleaning" it.

3/30/09 6:15 p.m. An elderly man having difficulties holding his pants up tried to cross the road at A Avenue and State Street.

3/30/09 9:15 p.m. A man reportedly acting suspicious in a hotel parking lot admitted he was nervous about returning to his room because he didn't want to be in trouble for being intoxicated.

4/1/09 8:29 p.m. A man tried to break things off with a woman he met on the Internet but she kept sending him texts anyway.

4/7/09 7:30 a.m. A dead duck was reported on Westview Drive. Standing next to it was a live duck.

4/7/09 1:06 p.m. A tall, skinny man walking, raised concern as he walked by a woman's house.

4/11/09 5:17 p.m. Two suspicious women carrying bags jumped into a vehicle headed toward Portland.

4/10/09 11:43 p.m. A woman believed her neighbor was blowing cold air into her apartment.

4/15/09 4:56 p.m. A father requested that police speak with his disrespectful son.

4/16/09 5:02 p.m. An 18-year-old girl refused to return a sweater she had borrowed.

4/17/09 12:04 p.m. A large truck is blocking parking spaces at a sandwich restaurant.

4/17/09 1:25 p.m. An elderly woman had difficulty parking her car at a supermarket.

4/17/09 3:59 p.m. A stranger walked into a woman's yard.

4/17/09 10:33 p.m. A suspect rang a doorbell and then ran away. The only evidence were some wet footprints on the step.

4/17/09 10:54 p.m. Tomato sauce and chocolate were found on a car at a supermarket.

4/20/09 10:35 p.m. Some bicyclists weren't using the bike lane and instead were blatantly riding in the road on South Shore Boulevard.

4/21/09 2:48 p.m. A man with a shaved head, in his late teens or early 20s, aimlessly strolled through a neighborhood for 30 minutes.

4/25/09 8:44 p.m. Restroom problems were reported at Millennium Plaza Park.

4/30/09 3:08 p.m. A person wearing a sandwich board was bothering students at

Lake Oswego High School.

4/30/09 7:40 p.m. A sick raccoon fell out of a tree then rolled under a shed where no one could reach it.

5/1/09 8:56 a.m. A momma duck and her ducklings were having trouble crossing Suncreek Drive.

5/3/09 2:09 p.m. A $5 bill at a golf course was thought to be counterfeit. However, it turned out to be genuine.

5/7/09 3:21 p.m. A girlfriend keeps doing crazy things, according to her boyfriend.

5/7/09 9:04 p.m. A person driving erratically on Fosberg Road flipped off an observer.

5/08/09 11:46 a.m. A woman flagged down an officer and said she was being stalked by dozens of people every time she went for a walk. Paranoia was not ruled out.

5/8/09 4:44 p.m. A man yelling at an apartment complex was told to knock it off.

5/9/09 6:15 a.m. A woman was disturbed by four loud bangs.

5/9/09 4:58 p.m. A low-hanging branch on Sixth Street caused concern.

5/9/09 12:42 a.m. A chipmunk named "Chip" ran away while on a visit from Washington state. It was suspected he was attempting to return home. Chip is wearing a blue collar with his license and tag, plus Chip is wearing a chip. Meghan, his owner, is hopeful of his return.

5/11/09 7:10 p.m. A man appeared on a woman's property even though he had absolutely no reason for being there.

5/11/09 11:28 p.m. A suspicious man walking in a neighborhood with a flashlight turned out to be a resident who had tripped a fuse and was trying to fix it.

5/12/09 5:24 p.m. An elderly man was swerving all over the road because he was eating while driving.

5/15/09 10:56 a.m. Two deer were prancing on Cherry Lane, and concern was expressed for their safety.

5/15/09 3:44 p.m. A verbal fracas erupted between parents and a daughter upset over being grounded. Peace was restored.

5/15/09 9:59 p.m. A drunken person has been falling into bushes, rolling over the sidewalk and skipping down the road.

5/20/09 4:37 p.m. A man's cellphone was reportedly taken from his house. However, he noted he had been packing and might have simply misplaced it.

5/20/09 10:07 p.m. A young girl was heard screaming from a house on West Bay Road. An investigation found she was cheering while watching "American Idol."

5/21/09 12:51 p.m. Suspicious people were seen inside the fence of a location. It turned out they were employees going to work.

5/23/09 1:50 p.m. An investigation of a reported loud party at an apartment on Jefferson Parkway found just two friends talking loudly.

5/23/09 4:24 p.m. Plants on the median on Boones Ferry and Country Club roads look like they could use some watering.

5/27/09 7:54 p.m. A suspicious looking salesman who claims to be from Comcast has reportedly visited several homes.

5/29/09 8:20 p.m. A man with a goatee was suspicious at Westlake Park.

5/31/09 11:12 a.m. A 16-year-old girl has locked herself in her bedroom, and her mother fears the girl is hatching plans to run away.

6/2/09 11:24 a.m. A group of people gathered around a 2-foot-long iguana found in a woman's yard. However, closer examination found the iguana to be a fake.

6/1/09 7:50 p.m. A nasty neighbor has been glaring and making faces at children riding their bicycles.

6/2/09 10:42 p.m. Unauthorized visitors living at an apartment complex for two weeks caused a woman to be "very upset."

6/3/09 9:46 a.m. Two people who seemed to be picking a lock had been hired to change the locks on a floral business.

6/3/09 12:08 p.m. A heavyset man wearing a black shirt while sitting in a vehicle, smoking a cigarette and listening to rap music was believed to be up to no good.

6/5/09 2:11 p.m. Four men in an SUV were staring at a woman.

6/5/09 9:34 p.m. What at first was thought to be a fight between 10 children turned out to be kids playing Frisbee.

6/6/09 8:57 p.m. A woman locked out by her husband responded by banging on the door, which was bothersome to a neighbor.

6/7/09 5:05 p.m. An employee at a local business was worried about a customer who was playing video games all the time.

6/8/09 8:56 a.m. A van reportedly packed full of solicitors on Wembley Park Road turned out to be a film crew.

6/8/09 10:39 a.m. A pizza delivery driver had to swerve sharply to avoid a Porsche that ran a red light. The sudden and unexpected action caused the pizzas to be ruined.

6/9/09 8:10 p.m. A woman was walking funny while carrying a dog.

6/10/09 12:40 a.m. A woman reported hearing coughing from beneath her house. However, an investigation failed to reveal a cougher.

6/10/09 9:39 a.m. A grandmother is concerned about her granddaughter's safety while associating with a person of questionable character.

6/11/09 5:07 p.m. A woman sought to file assault charges after her son was struck by a sunflower seed that was carelessly thrown by another boy.

6/12/09 5:43 p.m. A suspected domestic dispute turned out to be parents yelling at their children to get ready to leave.

6/11/09 7:47 p.m. Two brothers fought over a pizza after it was delivered.

6/12/09 8:33 p.m. Officers were in hot pursuit of a St. Bernard running loose down Chandler Road.

6/15/09 11:35 a.m. A suspicious-looking man who got out of a vehicle and set out an orange cone turned out to be a meter reader.

6/15/09 1:59 p.m. A man thought to be littering was just doing yard work for a friend.

6/16/09 11:47 a.m. Police helped a woman rescue a squirrel that appeared to be stuck in one of her patio chairs.

6/18/09 12:59 p.m. An 18-year-old son refused to give the car keys back to his mother.

6/18/09 5:10 p.m. A panhandler was begging too aggressively on State Street.

6/22/09 7:55 a.m. A man who took a nap in a van drove off before he could be questioned about his activity.

6/26/09 11:02 a.m. Neighbors keep coming into a woman's yard even though she never invites them.

6/27/09 12:21 a.m. A bag of potato chips was burned in a small fire.

6/29/09 11:23 a.m. A mean-spirited stepmother took away her stepson's cellphone and refused to return it.

6/29/09 10:35 a.m. A father is refusing to allow his 7-year-old daughter to use her cellphone.

6/29/09 3:31 p.m. A small crow, which appeared to be very young, has been under a boat trailer in a woman's driveway for three days. It is feared the little bird has been abandoned.

6/29/09 8:17 p.m. While driving a gold Mercedes, a teen girl was texting instead of paying attention to the road. A talk with her mother was strongly suggested.

6/30/09 2:29 p.m. A double car carrier trailer has been parked in front of a house for two days, and the man next door is highly upset because it's making it difficult to get out of his driveway.

6/30/09 11:43 p.m. Due to the suddenly strange behavior of her dog, a woman felt officers should come look around her house.

7/1/09 3:39 a.m. After a report of screaming at a residence on McVey Avenue, an officer defused the situation by assisting in the making of peanut butter-and-jelly sandwiches.

7/2/09 5:46 p.m. A man requested extra police patrols after a plastic flamingo was taken from his yard.

7/3/09 12:17 p.m. A suspicious man in a white hat on Meadows Road said he was looking for a Hair Club and then left in a white station wagon.

7/17/09 2:01 p.m. An attempt to capture a parrot was made on Hillshire Drive.

7/17/09 4:04 p.m. An employee at a convenience store charged a woman's card twice, then was rude to her when she pointed it out.

7/21/09 4:20 p.m. A woman complained that her upstairs neighbor had a bad smell. However, the odor turned out to be wafting from a nearby Dumpster.

7/26/09 10:02 p.m. Neighbors with a karaoke machine ignited a woman's chagrin.

7/27/09 11:51 a.m. A woman thinks she is being stalked but isn't sure.

7/28/09 9:15 p.m. A subject who appeared to be very drunk asked for food at a restaurant.

7/29/09 7:24 p.m. A man jumped in his car, peeling out and burning rubber. In his wake he left a distinct odor of marijuana.

8/3/09 9:10 a.m. A driver was weaving all over Boones Ferry Road and Kruse Way. It was determined he was not drunk, just driving badly.

8/5/09 7:37 p.m. A woman reported someone was following her and putting brown water on her plants.

8/9/09 10 a.m. A complaint was lodged about loud singing from a location. It turned out to be a church group that was breaking up.

8/6/09 12:21 a.m. A group of eight to 10 teens, all more than 18 years old, were dancing in the cul-de-sac near a school. They were warned about the noise and told to go home.

8/9/09 9:57 p.m. A strange object, possibly a raccoon, fell off a woman's roof and then her deck.

8/10/09 7:57 p.m. A rude neighbor honked his horn.

8/11/09 7:14 p.m. In what was reported as a burglary in progress, a Realtor was showing a home to some viewers.

8/12/09 3:57 p.m. After reporting someone had broken into her residence, a woman discovered that the culprit was her daughter.

8/13/09 6:59 p.m. A man locked his brother out of his apartment and refused to let him in.

8/17/09 6:36 a.m. A peacock was in the road at Boones Ferry Road and West Sunset Drive.

8/17/09 11:50 a.m. A burglary suspect turned out to be a cleaning lady. All was OK.

8/18/09 6:05 p.m. Following being trespassed from a location, a man came back, puked, then ran away.

8/19/09 8:38 p.m. An odd smell in a neighborhood turned out to be people cooking s'mores.

8/20/09 8:33 p.m. A driver weaving all over the road turned out to be an inept student driver.

8/24/09 12:53 p.m. A man supposedly harassing a woman by ringing her doorbell and banging on her walls was actually a PGE technician installing a new meter.

8/24/09 5:06 p.m. A female has been sitting in the backseat of an old car all day.

8/25/09 3:03 p.m. A man cannot go out for a walk without a local dog running up to him and barking at him.

8/31/09 8:58 p.m. A neighborhood has been hit by a wave of children ringing doorbells and running.

9/1/09 11:08 p.m. Three juveniles jumped off the roof of a restaurant. When asked why by officers, they said they were "extreme running."

9/1/09 11:18 p.m. Five naked people in an apartment pool were being obnoxiously loud.

9/3/09 3:07 p.m. Standing in front of a school was a man with dreadlocks, a white T-shirt and baggy jeans. Possibly a rapper.

9/3/09 8:17 p.m. Neighbors have been swearing at each other in an ongoing dispute.

9/4/09 6:17 p.m. What was reported as a burglary turned out to be bakers baking bread inside of a bakery.

9/9/09 11:29 a.m. A man walking near Waluga Park was heard singing loudly and spouting obscenities.

9/14/09 4:10 p.m. An elderly man acted confused at a pizza restaurant.

9/15/09 3:22 p.m. A man with a rolled-up newspaper went into a store and refused to leave when asked. It is believed he is homeless.

9/15/09 4:47 p.m. An old lady has been throwing plums at her neighbor.

9/15/09 8:04 p.m. A family fight in a fast-food restaurant was quieted by official intervention.

9/16/09 1:44 p.m. A woman complained that her neighbor's garage sale had been going on for far too long.

9/17/09 8:58 p.m. A short, heavy, suspicious man was advised to leave a supermarket after he was observed leaning against a wall.

9/22/09 11:50 p.m. Because he was drunk and unconscious, a man could not respond when his neighbors pounded on his door due to the loud, depressing music he was playing.

9/23/09 4:41 p.m. It sure looks like people are doing drugs at an apartment complex where a vehicle shows up every evening, after the office is closed, and is greeted by folks from the building.

9/24/09 7:28 p.m. A man's 10-year-old son was yelling about not being able to get on a computer.

9/27/09 9:31 a.m. A car parked for church was blocking a driveway on Beasley Way. Officers determined the car was parked legally, but the churchgoer moved the vehicle to keep the peace.

9/27/09 4:48 p.m. A woman called police because every time she goes to her brother's house his girlfriend calls and disturbs them.

9/27/09 8:19 p.m. A mother and her 10-year-old son were in a verbal dispute regarding the TV.

9/27/09 9:19 p.m. A suspicious person in a white sedan wearing new work gloves claimed he was lost in the 1200 block of Rockinghorse Lane.

9/28/09 11:37 p.m. A bride-to-be was playing loud music in order to find a song for her wedding. She was advised of the complaint.

9/30/09 9:52 p.m. A woman received a series of hang-up calls in the evenings over the past week.

10/1/09 2:07 p.m. Two men were going from door to door and acting peculiar.

10/2/09 7:15 p.m. A woman yelled at three juvenile skateboarders as they rolled down a hill. They yelled back at her.

10/7/09 9:29 a.m. A girlfriend had a nightmare, which her boyfriend thought was a seizure. A check proved that indeed it was a nightmare.

10/8/09 2:17 p.m. A female driver hanging out at an elementary school told officers she was checking out the school for her kids next year.

10/8/09 4:15 p.m. A woman refused to leave city hall for over an hour.

10/12/09 5:10 p.m. A solicitor did soliciting at a home with a "No Soliciting sign," then requested to use the telephone — which turned out to be a long-distance call.

10/14/09 12:02 p.m. Groups of juveniles were crossing at an intersection in such a careless manner that it caused motorists to slam on their brakes.

10/13/09 4:19 p.m. Firewood was stacked in a possibly unsafe manner after a homeowner cut down a tree.

10/15/09 8:09 a.m. A neighbor feels it is about time that a man selling his Porsche moves the car.

10/16/09 9:37 p.m. In a case of intense littering, bags from a fast-food hamburger restaurant were dumped all over a driveway.

10/17/09 6 p.m. A woman reported that a suspicious vehicle had been parked in front of her house all day long. It turned out to be a moving van.

10/20/09 9:32 a.m. Bird droppings on cars on Second Street are a big problem, and a woman thinks she knows the person responsible for it.

10/21/09 11:38 p.m. A runaway 15-year-old girl is threatening to go to downtown Portland or even Canada.

10/22/09 5:15 p.m. A possibly sick or injured raccoon eluded the efforts of a woman trying to catch it in her backyard. After observing the raccoon up a tree, an officer noted it appeared to be fine.

10/23/09 2:24 p.m. A gray rabbit with black, floppy ears has been hopping around a front yard on Palisades Crest Drive the past few days.

10/25/09 8:07 p.m. A mother and her 10-year-old daughter had a verbal fracas after the girl lost her glasses.

10/30/09 6:16 p.m. A female and child in a stroller not dressed appropriately for the weather have been sitting on a corner for the past 90 minutes.

10/31/09 8:15 p.m. Six or seven female teens were writing on fences with chalk.

10/31/09 9:27 p.m. A man dodged what he thought was an egg thrown by a kid. It turned out to be a pinecone.

11/1/09 3:01 a.m. A reportedly drunken woman on the street turned out to be a sober man.

11/2/09 2:39 p.m. A driver reportedly had an open container while refueling his car. However, it was found to contain water, not booze.

11/4/09 4:43 p.m. Six teens yelling "Michael, stop it" were observed at a park on Southwest Childs Road.

11/4/09 9:10 p.m. Six teens using a flashlight and thought to be yelling at passing motorists on Botticelli and Touchstone were found to be on their way back from church.

11/9/09 10:33 p.m. A woman is calling and texting a man despite his wishes for her to stop.

11/10/09 4:32 p.m. A man with a loud chainsaw has been riling his neighbors.

11/13/09 4:41 p.m. Six juveniles were being rude to employees at a chicken restaurant.

11/14/09 3:37 p.m. A woman claimed her cat was inside an empty house that was up for sale and had no occupants. Indeed, when officers opened the door, the cat came out.

11/16/09 1:51 p.m. A woman reported her ex-mother-in-law is saying bad things about her to her 6-year-old daughter.

11/16/09 2:22 p.m. Noisy neighbors at an apartment complex have been slamming doors and yelling, especially when they're drunk.

11/18/09 4:35 p.m. An inconsiderate neighbor is putting his recycling items into his neighbor's recycling bin.

11/19/09 5:58 p.m. A man loading wood into his van said he was planning to build doghouses. It turned out he was telling the truth.

12/1/09 9:20 a.m. An intruder was suspected when a door to a house was left open and a toilet was running. A check found that the toilet had a leaky valve.

12/4/09 4:18 p.m. Drugs were believed to be the reason for a man stumbling down the street, picking up objects to examine them and then skipping down the road.

12/8/09 10:07 a.m. What was thought to be suspicious voices in a house turned out to be a pest control team taking care of paperwork.

12/13/09 1:23 a.m. A suspect from an egging incident in September was seen at the scene of a past crime. However, no new crime was detected.

12/19/09 9:06 p.m. A husband and wife got into an argument after he accused her of acting weird.

12/23/09 11:41 p.m. A woman who gave a man a ride home is starting to feel uncomfortable and would like to get rid of him.

12/24/09 12:27 a.m. Uninvited party guests started drinking vodka and tequila.

12/27/09 11:11 a.m. An investigation by an officer found that a report on the demise of a raccoon was premature.

12/31/09 12:54 p.m. While taking down Christmas decorations for a friend, a man noticed a suspicious figure on the second floor. It was a cardboard cutout.

2010

1/2/10 8 a.m. Garbage cans are being tipped over at a convenience store by a tip-toeing man.

1/8/10 1:51 p.m. A panhandler has been successful in obtaining some large handouts from customers at a convenience store, but this is making the store's manager nervous.

1/9/10 8:43 p.m. A husband slammed his wife's hand in a dishwasher and locked her in the laundry room. The couple is getting divorced.

1/13/10 11:10 p.m. A man went over and yelled at his neighbor for talking too loudly.

1/18/10 4:44 p.m. A man is being made uncomfortable by a neighbor carrying a big stick.

1/18/10 4:37 p.m. A wife tossed her estranged husband's clothes into the garbage after he came in and asked to wash them. Before leaving, he poked her with his keys.

1/20/10 7:25 p.m. Long-haired solicitors were working on Foothills Drive.

1/23/10 3:49 p.m. Four or five cars full of people arrived at a park, and one of the people was dressed head to toe in a bright blue sorcerer's outfit and pointy hat. An investigation by a park ranger found that they were taking senior photos.

1/24/10 3:21 a.m. Someone was knocking on a woman's door and ringing the bell for 15 minutes. It was the woman's son.

1/25/10 10:44 a.m. A member of the community was frantic after trying to check on a 91-year-old resident and not finding her. It turned out she had gone to the wrong house.

Hitting the big time

Jan. 28, 2010

An excerpt from the Lake Oswego Review's police blotter was read Monday night on NBC's Jay Leno Show.

The talk show host does a "Headlines" segment every Monday, showing headlines, text and photos from around the nation that tickle his funny bone.

The smirking Leno displayed a page from the Review and read the following:

"A Lake Oswegan woman spent 20 minutes talking dirty on the telephone before she realized the caller was not her boyfriend. She later contacted police to report the incident."

After reading it, a tickled Leno looked at his studio audience and asked:

"Why? What do you say? Why would you call the police? ... [Do you want to get them to call the guy to say] Hey, call me back!"

2/1/10 4:42 p.m. A woman's children, aged 7 and 10, are stealing from her. She requested that a police officer talk to them.

2/2/10 3:54 p.m. After being asked to leave The Club, a man returned the following night accompanied by his attorney. The banned man gave a "death stare" to the person who complained about him.

2/3/10 7:44 p.m. A woman clad only in her underwear refused to go inside, even though she admitted to being cold.

2/6/10 12:54 p.m. A very friendly, yellow dog with short legs has been running in an area for a week.

2/7/10 8:52 p.m. A reckless driver going all over the road apologized to an officer for poor driving, which was caused by a car full of intoxicated people giving erratic directions.

2/8 8:06 a.m. A disoriented elderly woman was walking up Carman Drive while carrying a bag of popcorn.

2/11/10 1:03 p.m. A condo owner has been the target of pinecones thrown by a neighbor.

2/12/10 6:42 p.m. A man wearing black clothing was staggering onto the roadway. He was urged to walk on the sidewalk.

2/14/10 8:45 p.m. A messy apartment ignited a yelling and screaming match between three people.

2/14/10 4 p.m. A severed foot found in the woods at an apartment complex turned out to be a toy.

2/15/10 3:39 p.m. Two boys and two girls were running in front of traffic and spitting on passing bicyclists.

2/16/10 8:29 a.m. A man looked out into his yard and saw a coyote.

2/17/10 10:11 a.m. Drug deals are possibly being made at a convenience store because cars keep driving in and out of the location – or perhaps they are just customers.

2/17/10 10:11 a.m. Former neighbors are suspected of opening a packet of ketchup and putting it on a child's bedroom window.

2/23/10 8:13 a.m. A mysterious man was seen sitting on top of a child's playhouse.

3/1/10 1:12 p.m. In suspicious activity, people have been stopping at a flowerbed and looking through it.

3/1/10 7:11 p.m. Sliced ham was placed all over a car.

3/2/10 10:03 p.m. A man in a tan van for 30 minutes is giving off suspicious vibes.

3/3/10 4:42 p.m. A black Rottweiler approached a young girl. The dog appeared confused and was walking in circles.

3/3/10 5:43 p.m. A golden Labradoodle was running at large. It was distinguished by the cone of shame on its head.

3/8/10 2:22 p.m. An ex-boyfriend stood on the porch of his ex-girlfriend's house, crying and pleading to get his belongings back. Despite his anguish, she refused to open the door. He finally left when he saw her dialing 911.

3/12/10 3:11 p.m. A renter looked up and saw that the drapes were missing in her rental home.

3/13/10 7:37 a.m. Four stray goats were rounded up and returned to their home on Rosemont Road.

3/17/10 12:24 p.m. A Lab ran into a woman's yard, chased her cat into the house, then ran all over her house and jumped on her furniture, leaving it wet and dirty. The dog's owner was cited for his pet's outrageous behavior.

3/18/10 12:03 p.m. A woman climbed out of her gold Honda Civic and smacked a man, then left the scene on foot.

3/19/10 1:12 p.m. A dispute broke out over the installation of a curtain.

3/21/10 5:59 p.m. A man was seen running behind some brush near a church. An investigation by an officer discovered that the subject and his son were hiding in the bushes to scare the mom.

3/25/10 8:05 a.m. A thin, unfriendly man with a buzz haircut is standing alongside A Avenue.

3/26/10 6:10 p.m. A suspicious man was seen removing a stone from his shoe.

4/8/10 10:35 a.m. Two girls engaged in mutual combat at Lakeridge High School.

4/9/10 6:37 p.m. Advice was sought about a possible Vietnamese gang doing a phone survey.

4/12/10 1:25 a.m. A man who couldn't find his glasses called 911 for police assistance.

4/16/10 10:47 a.m. A woman sought permission to carry Mace to protect herself from coyotes.

4/16/10 10:45 a.m. A woman reported she is receiving letters addressing her as "mister." She prefers being addressed as "doctor," not "mister."

4/20/10 3:45 p.m. Two raccoons were frolicking in a woman's yard on Greensborough Court. One raccoon departed, but the other did not.

4/20/10 5:27 p.m. Six teenage boys gathered together to smoke cigarettes.

4/23/10 4:26 p.m. Attempts by officers to catch a goose at George Rogers Park were unsuccessful.

4/24/10 5:08 p.m. A child was walking around with a prop knife stuck in his head.

4/26/10 9:57 a.m. A 15-year-old boy walked down the street barefoot after an argument with his parents.

4/26/10 11:39 a.m. A single-engine plane flew far too low for the comfort for a resident on Ridgecrest Drive.

4/28/10 7:06 a.m. Traffic was slowed by a woman in an electric wheelchair who was drinking a large glass of wine.

4/28/10 4:08 p.m. A screaming 5- or 6-year-old boy was forced to sit in a chair by his grandmother.

4/28/10 7:57 p.m. An angry-looking crowd of people and dogs were seen heading up Country Club Road seemingly chasing somebody. They turned out to be a runners club.

4/30/10 8:16 a.m. A gallon milk jug with 2 inches of milk was left on a woman's porch.

5/3/10 10:38 a.m. A fight appeared to have broken out in an apartment where screaming was heard. It sounded like people were beating each other up. A check by officers found that it was a group of young males watching a soccer match.

5/4/10 7:15 a.m. A small, brown chicken is missing. "Fowl" play is suspected.

5/8/10 10:27 a.m. An 11-year-old boy was being spied upon through a window in his home by suspicious-looking men in dark suits. They were representatives of the Jehovah's Witness Church.

5/12/10 10:41 a.m. An ex-girlfriend broke into a house and left a fifth of whiskey and a picture.

5/12/10 3:03 a.m. A missing husband was discovered in his own home.

5/16/10 11:39 a.m. What was originally thought to be a bloodily wounded deer or lamb turned out be a red dinosaur balloon.

5/21/10 6:53 p.m. A dispute between a daughter and her mother broke out at a therapist's office.

5/25/10 5:48 p.m. A box of dark chocolates was among the items taken in a house burglary.

5/25/10 2:58 a.m. A driver using a rental car cannot figure out how to turn off the lights.

5/26/10 5:01 p.m. A customer called in a large order for a family birthday party and wanted a $950 tip added to a credit card. This struck the restaurant staff as highly unusual.

5/30/10 7:51 a.m. A man went to his mailbox and found a large potted plant in it.

5/31/10 3:22 p.m. A report of geese attacking a duckling on State Street was called in. However, an officer arrived on the scene to find the critters were playing nicely.

6/4/10 8:14 p.m. Six disruptive juveniles went to an ice cream store and started screaming. Also, they didn't buy any ice cream.

6/5/10 9:15 p.m. Officers responded to a house with sounds of breaking things and yelling, and they discovered a child refusing to go to bed.

6/5/10 11:43 p.m. Cheez Whiz and peanut butter were spread over somebody's Volvo.

6/7/10 9:36 a.m. The words "ha ha" were spray-painted on the side of a bank.

6/12/10 6:07 p.m. A chair made from cardboard in a dumpster was used by a man while waiting for his friend to get off work at Kentucky Fried Chicken.

6/15/10 10:57 p.m. What at first appeared to be a drug deal turned out to be the passing of a blackberry pie in a bag.

6/21/10 12:09 a.m. Somebody claiming to be the devil made a prank phone call.

6/23/10 9:48 a.m. A man is seeking advice about putting a "trap" on his car so thieves will quit breaking into it.

6/26/10 2:42 p.m. An unruly restaurant customer threw salads and pushed two employees. Naturally, she was then removed.

6/27/10 9:42 p.m. A very large turtle departed with all possible haste after jumping off an embankment along Iron Mountain Boulevard.

7/1/10 3:27 p.m. In an attempt to rescue an injured duck, a woman jumped into a river. Officers had to coax her back to shore.

7/4/10 1:20 a.m. A man who was thought to be unconscious told rescue workers he was fine. He was simply refusing to let his wife wake him up.

7/8/10 8:01 p.m. A heavy, bald man wearing Bermuda shorts was pushing a bicycle and seemed disoriented and "creepy."

7/12/10 3:47 p.m. Neighbors are saying that peacocks on West Sunset Drive should be kept on leashes like other pets.

7/14/10 5:40 p.m. Constant loud partying by neighbors is causing a woman to become physically ill from lack of sleep.

7/15/10 1:47 p.m. A man is seeking advice on how loud and how long his son can play his drums in their garage.

7/18/10 9:19 p.m. Raccoons were spotted on a woman's fence. She was informed this was not unusual.

7/22/10 6:52 p.m. Some ducklings caught in a storm drain on Parkview Drive caused their mama duck to walk around in an agitated manner.

Ask a cop

Dec. 26, 2013

"Is the police log printed in the Review real?"

ANSWER: The Review receives a copy of our daily log which has personal information redacted. From this information, the Review then "fills in the gaps" if you will and creates something more colorful to read than the basic information printed in our daily log. So, while the incidents are real, the story surrounding the event is filled in by writers at the Review for your reading pleasure.

— *Lt. Doug Treat*

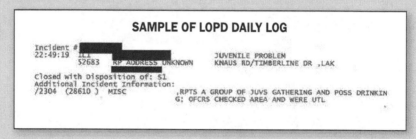

SAMPLE OF LOPD DAILY LOG

```
Incident #
22:49:19  ▓▓▓
          52683   RP ADDRESS UNKNOWN      JUVENILE PROBLEM
                                          KNAUS RD/TIMBERLINE DR ,LAK

Closed with Disposition of: 51
Additional Incident Information:
/2304  (28610 )  MISC           ,RPTS A GROUP OF JUVS GATHERING AND POSS DRINKIN
                                G; OFCRS CHECKED AREA AND WERE UTL
```

[Editor's note: While it's true that police reporter Cliff Newell will look for not-so-serious examples of life in Lake Oswego as reported to the police to include in the Review's police log, he is not making material up. He merely is giving a light touch to a few items each week in the log's miscellaneous category.]

7/23/10 4:27 p.m. A swarm of wasps was keeping a woman trapped inside of her home.

7/24/10 12:22 a.m. A woman's apartment was broken into and several items were taken. The woman suspects her daughter did it because the only items taken belonged to her.

7/29/10 9:08 a.m. A person came into a woman's home during the night, made breakfast, then departed. Nothing appeared to have been taken, but dirty dishes were left behind.

7/26/10 11:10 a.m. A stranger showed up in a backyard on Crestline Court and remarked, "I must have the wrong house."

7/26/10 11:25 a.m. A widow is searching for the car her late husband left parked somewhere in Lake Oswego.

7/27/10 10:21 a.m. A woman became upset when she thought her apartment neighbor had sneaked into her garden to steal some vegetables.

7/28/10 12:24 p.m. Five chickens suddenly appeared on a man's patio on Glen Haven Road.

7/29/10 3:53 p.m. Jumping juveniles are aggressively using the dolphin statues at Oswego Pointe for their airborne excursions.

8/1/10 3:02 p.m. A son stands accused of stealing a couple's cat and staying in their house while there were away.

8/2/10 1:12 p.m. A boy admitted lying about his father being a police officer.

8/3/10 7:54 a.m. A suspect tried to break into a house by getting through the cat door.

8/18/10 5:21 p.m. Eight teens were seen at Westlake Park playing on toys meant for much smaller children.

8/18/10 10:04 p.m. A loud party playing loud music was met with a loud complaint.

8/21/10 6:45 p.m. A woman rebuffed a party invitation from a man wearing an orange-striped shirt.

8/25/10 9:31 p.m. A man fell asleep in the grass and missed his ride.

9/4/10 8:22 p.m. An ongoing dispute between neighbors has culminated in one of them throwing the other neighbor's slipper into a swamp.

9/9/10 2:34 p.m. A white Ford Escape with the labeling of "The Killers" aroused worry on Country Club Road. However, it was determined the vehicle belonged to an extermination company.

8/30/10 1:28 p.m. Long weeds on a property are causing long faces on neighbors.

9/11/10 6:21 p.m. Adults scurrying back and forth on State Street while carrying envelopes were found to be on a scavenger hunt.

9/12/10 3:24 a.m. A missing wife was found asleep downstairs by her husband. He had called police when she had not returned from a trip to a restaurant on State Street.

9/19/10 2:14 p.m. Kids were taking coins from a fountain at Millennium Plaza Park.

9/23/10 8:17 p.m. A female who has been eating off other people's plates and then not paying for the food has been cut off by an acquaintance.

9/26/10 9:12 p.m. When a man called to check on his parents they kept hanging up on him. They are OK, they just don't want to talk to him.

9/27/10 4:39 p.m. A creepy college student selling magazines made a woman uncomfortable with his sales pitch and personal appearance (including earrings in both ears).

Ask a cop

March 27, 2014

"All cliches aside, does VooDoo Doughnuts really have the best doughnuts in Oregon?"

ANSWER: I have been a police officer for a little over 20 years now and we all know the stigma that follows us with doughnuts and, because of that, I had a 17 year streak of not eating a doughnut. Not a single one — not even a doughnut hole. That was because I was forced to buy doughnuts for a meeting in uniform in 1996. Not just a few  doughnuts, but two dozen doughnuts. You can imagine my horror as parents pointed to me and told their children, "See police really do eat doughnuts!" However, that streak ended last summer when my wife forced me to take a bite of her bacon maple bar from VooDoo Doughnuts. It was well worth the wait — mmmm. But your question is if VooDoo Doughnuts are really the best in the state. Being a police officer automatically makes me an authority on doughnuts and having sampled doughnuts from Dunkin' Donuts, 7-Eleven, various Mom 'n' Pop doughnut stores, organic doughnuts, gluten-free doughnuts (Kyra's Bake Shop makes the absolute best), whatever that was sitting on the back counter that looked like a doughnut, I can unequivocally say that VooDoo Doughnuts has some of the best doughnuts in the state. Especially their chocolate old-fashioned and blueberry doughnuts ... although you will probably never catch me eating one, at least not in public. And if you're going to visit VooDoo Doughnuts, be sure to visit their East side location in Portland — there's never a line ... at least in my experience!

— *Lt. Doug Treat*

9/27/10 8:13 p.m. The awful smell coming from a vehicle turned out to be a malodorous sleeping man and there was no sign of foul play. Just foul odor.

9/28/10 1:18 a.m. Suspicious sounds in the night were heard by a woman living in an apartment on Kerr Parkway. When she opened her door, she found a bag of spaghetti sauce.

10/4/10 3:41 p.m. In a case of convenience store rage, one woman pushed another woman out of the way as she was trying to grab milk and then yelled profanities at her.

10/5/10 6:11 p.m. Death proved to be the reason a squirrel was not moving under a tree.

10/7/10 10:02 a.m. Questions were raised about the competence of a pizza delivery driver.

10/8/10 11:50 a.m. A woman became frightened when a man got out of a vehicle carrying red sticks that appeared to be dynamite. Fortunately, they were only flares.

10/18/10 1:16 p.m. After searching high and wide for her lost poodle, a woman looked low and found it under the porch.

10/19/10 12:31 p.m. Suspicion was raised about an 11-year-old boy selling paper flowers to raise money for his soccer team.

10/20/10 9:59 a.m. A bike rider rode so close to a female pedestrian that he brushed her sleeve.

10/20/10 11:14 a.m. After collapsing in a yard on Atwater Lane, a sick coyote suddenly perked up and ran off into the woods.

10/26/10 4:27 p.m. A landlord entered a tenant's room during the night and took several things, including his dog.

10/28/10 11:03 p.m. A cat was threatened by a person wielding scissors.

11/3/10 9:06 p.m. A crash and bang followed by barking dogs resulted after a raccoon knocked over a garbage can on Iron Mountain Boulevard.

11/3/10 8:55 p.m. A suspicious female and male lurking at a dentist's office turned out to be the janitors.

11/3/10 9:12 p.m. An apparent break-in at a residence on Botticelli Street turned out to be a mixed-up person who went to the wrong door. It was called an honest mistake.

11/3/10 9:56 p.m. Two customers — possibly thinking they were in Amsterdam — were enjoying marijuana along with their coffee at a cafe on Boones Ferry Road.

11/18/10 2:38 p.m. A coyote that apparently lives in the area of Amberwood Circle and Westlake Drive has taken to using the sidewalk.

11/10/10 5:04 p.m. A missing 5-year-old boy was discovered on the couch of his home.

11/16/10 10:55 a.m. A tall, skinny man wearing a baseball cap keeps knocking on a woman's apartment door. He won't say who he is and he won't leave.

11/16/10 9:05 p.m. A supposed fight between a man and a woman at an apartment turned out to be only adults playing with children.

11/19/10 2:46 p.m. A squabble between roommates broke out over who was responsible for their dirty kitchen.

11/21/10 1:48 p.m. An 11-year-old daughter began screaming after she was not allowed to use Facebook.

11/23/10 6:44 p.m. A 24-year-old son is refusing to leave home, so his mother called the police on him.

11/24/10 2:20 p.m. A woman says she is getting thrown out by her landlord, who she claims is unstable, emotional, bad tempered and scary.

11/24/10 6:44 p.m. Raccoons trapped in a storm drain were rescued by LOPD officers.

11/25/10 11:30 a.m. An American flag was hanging upside down at a bank. This mistake was hastily rectified by a maintenance worker.

11/30/10 7:26 a.m. A woman says that someone comes to her house each day at 5 a.m. and sings to her over a loudspeaker. The singer has yet to be found.

12/1/10 5:20 p.m. Worries were aroused on Kingsgate Road when the voice of a child was heard crying, "Stop it!" An investigation found that it was a 12-year-old boy upset about pizza.

12/10/10 9:13 p.m. A dead animal found under a woman's TV cabinet was carefully removed by an officer.

12/13/10 12:48 p.m. A man with a cup of coffee walked into a bank and started asking customers for money.

12/21/10 8:48 a.m. People were seen using a ladder to go in and out of a room at Motel 6.

12/21/10 3:31 p.m. A 15-year-old dialed 911 because he was upset that his computer was taken away.

12/27/10 9:33 a.m. A stocky but fast dog managed to elude an officer in a chase down Lake Bay Court.

12/28/10 7:42 p.m. A female who may be high on more than life just left an ice cream store.

12/30/10 11:41 p.m. An ex-boyfriend cannot understand how his ex-girlfriend got into his apartment since he had the locks changed.

12/31/10 12:34 p.m. What first seemed to be a case of sexual assault, turned out to be consensual sex between a couple in a vehicle parked on Centerpointe Drive. The male participant grinned at the woman who reported the incident as she walked by.

Firefighters save squirrel's life – and tail

June 14, 2013

Lake Oswego firefighters have to be ready for anything, as they rescue a squirrel caught in razor wire on a fence. It was firefighter Andrew Hedges who first noticed a squirrel whose tail was stuck in razor wire on top of a fence and was unable to move. Hedges was joined by firefighting comrades Dick Griffin and Jim Doane, who studied and evaluated the situation. They had to work fast because the desperate squirrel was starting to chew on its own tail in an effort to get loose from the nasty predicament.

The firefighters grabbed a ladder. As Hedges held onto the squirrel, Griffin untangled the furry critter's tail. The freed squirrel scurried back into nature.

"The squirrel was very much stuck and wouldn't have been able to get free otherwise," Gert Zoutendijk, Lake Oswego Fire Marshal, said.

Animal rescue is one of the Lake Oswego Fire Department's many duties. The exception is when cats are caught up trees; those operations are left to cat rescue experts like Bob Stewert of Lake Oswego. In the past, firefighters have rescued dogs trapped on cliffs, cats in chimneys and deer caught in mud.

2011

1/1/11 5:58 p.m. A male and female with a large, empty garbage bag showed up at a house and asked for Alex. When asked who they were, the couple departed with haste.

1/1/11 6:49 p.m. A woman called and said she was feeling funny after smoking marijuana.

1/2/11 1:44 a.m. After locking herself out of her house on Lower Drive, a woman is stranded on her back deck. Pop-A-Lock is not answering her calls.

1/3/11 12:17 p.m. Before help could arrive, a sick cat in a backyard disappeared.

1/3/11 6:14 p.m. Drunkenness was suspected when a driver motoring down Country Club Road swerved into a bike path and into oncoming traffic. However, this erratic performance was due to children arguing in the vehicle.

1/7/11 3:40 p.m. A car filled with too many juveniles and not enough safety belts just left Oak Creek Elementary School.

1/8/11 6:51 p.m. Concern was aroused when a woman arrived home and found an unfamiliar car in her driveway. It was a lost motorist.

1/11/11 7:28 p.m. A woman is worried about her 80-year-old husband walking their dog under icy conditions because he fell while doing it last week.

1/13/11 2:28 a.m. What appeared to be someone breaking into a condo on Lower Drive turned out to be a woman who locked herself out.

1/14/11 8:52 p.m. A female said she was laying in the middle of the road because she had been hit by a vehicle. However, she did manage to get up and walk away.

1/14/11 9:34 p.m. A man's marijuana use caused an argument between his brother and his parents.

1/18/11 7:34 p.m. A suspicious female driving a red vehicle attempted to abandon two dogs in Tualatin. An investigation found she was merely exercising her canines.

1/18/11 4:03 p.m. A teenager ran amok in a house, smashing up furniture and putting a hole in the bedroom door. His mother is displeased.

1/19/11 10:32 a.m. A woman at Hallinan Elementary School believes she is being stalked by a driver in a green car. Not only that, she thinks she is being stalked by a lot of people who are part of a stalking organization.

1/22/11 12:13 p.m. A man is threatening to break into a woman's residence to take a shower and pick up some clean clothes.

1/23/11 7:01 p.m. A customer at El Ranchito restaurant left without paying her tab. However, she did leave her purse in a booth.

1/23/11 10:06 p.m. A boy says he is afraid to go home because his brother is slapping him.

1/24/11 7:06 a.m. A large concrete flower pot was put into a parking space in front of a coffee shop on First Street.

1/27/11 9:02 p.m. When a couple finally answered a late-night doorbell, they looked outside and found their car had been Saran Wrapped.

1/31/11 9:22 a.m. A woman was alarmed by the sounds of her downstairs bathroom fan going on and off and of somebody snapping their fingers. It turned out to be her husband who had arrived home unexpectedly.

2/1/11 5:12 p.m. A woman called to say she was being held against her will in the X-ray department at Providence Milwaukie.

2/1/11 5:40 p.m. A male who allowed his spaniel puppy to run off-leash yelled at a woman to control her dog. She did not appreciate his blatant hypocrisy.

2/1/11 6:37 p.m. An SUV with its lights on drove directly in front of a business on Meadows Road. Employees were afraid to leave. However, it turned out to be customers in the van.

2/1/11 9:33 p.m. A possible UFO was sighted over 62nd Avenue and Southwest Southwood Drive. The strange flying object had a bright light and crisscrossed lights on its bottom and was spotted several times.

2/3/11 8:34 a.m. A paper deliveryman was found sleeping in his van, parked near Albertsons on Boones Ferry, after completing his work for the day.

2/3/11 5:16 p.m. The sound of a neighbor weeping and sounding despondent worried some folks at Ridgeview Condos.

2/4/11 12:13 p.m. A woman's teenage son traded the family vehicle for one he saw on Craigslist.

2/5/11 11:17 a.m. A mother walked by Westridge Elementary with one baby on her back and two children, wearing only pajamas, on leashes.

2/7/11 8:43 p.m. An unknown man showed up at Bryant Elementary School and started using a TV camera. It was determined to be KGW filming a story.

2/9/11 2 p.m. A suspicious person dressed in black was observed entering U.S. Bank on Kruse Oaks Drive. It was an employee.

2/11/11 1:27 p.m. A church is praying that a belligerent transient will take his presence to another denomination.

2/15/11 5:16 a.m. In an early morning emergency, a woman's bathroom door was stuck shut. Officers unstuck it.

2/17/11 5:13 p.m. A litterbug is putting tissues and tissue boxes all over a complex on North Shore Road and on State Street.

2/18/11 7:44 p.m. In a case of toilet terrorism, four juveniles in a Toyota 4Runner knocked over a porta potty at the junction of Centerwood Street and Indian Creek Drive.

2/20/11 3:15 a.m. A prowler turned out to be a drunken son searching for a place to sleep.

2/20/11 9:13 p.m. People are tripping over a large phonebook that was delivered to a man's house.

2/22/11 1:04 p.m. A confused-looking man started to change his clothes inside of a fast-food restaurant. He was a mixed martial arts competitor.

2/24/11 9:47 a.m. A juvenile admitted to throwing snowballs at cars, but promised he would never do it again.

2/27/11 11:53 p.m. A swerving car stopped, and a man, carrying a flashlight and holding a bag, ran out of some bushes and jumped into the vehicle.

3/3/11 2:55 p.m. Tenants at an apartment are bitter about a renter getting a handicapped parking permit when he does not deserve it.

3/3/11 3:22 p.m. Feces instead of gold was received in a package by a man who tried to purchase a valuable coin on eBay.

3/5/11 2:10 p.m. A driver was weaving through traffic not because he was drunk, but because he was trying to read something.

3/8/11 2:21 p.m. Two 5-year-olds rode their scooters onto a busy street, and they were not even wearing helmets. As it turned out, the tiny twosome had snuck away from their mother. She has now moved them to the backyard.

3/8/11 5:24 p.m. A solicitor informed a homeowner that a "No Soliciting" sign meant nothing to him.

3/16/11 11:13 a.m. A couple lied about their neighbor being spied upon by the FBI for the past three months.

3/24/11 1:37 p.m. An 11-year-old son threw a bottle of urine on his father, who is naturally upset.

3/26/11 12:26 a.m. Teens shot a marshmallow at a woman's vehicle on A Avenue.

3/29/11 7:45 p.m. A redheaded woman, aged 40 to 60, wearing a white hat, coat and boots, came walking down another woman's front steps on Village Park Lane and put her newspapers by her door. "We like to keep our neighborhood tidy," the redhead said.

4/6/11 3:58 p.m. A man was sleeping so soundly inside a vehicle that he failed to respond to knocking on his windows by a concerned passerby.

4/7/11 8:04 a.m. A suspicious person with a shovel entering Cookes Butte Park was a city employee clearing off the pathways.

4/8/11 11:18 a.m. A man with a "spinning head" was acting suspiciously at a store on Pilkington Road.

4/10/11 12:37 p.m. A woman's special rocks were spray-painted yellow by a city crew on Hampton Court.

4/12/11 3:38 p.m. A man with no pants on disturbed a woman on Parkview Drive.

4/13/11 9:59 a.m. An errant tri-colored beagle named Daisy has been found and returned to its home on Clara Court, where the dog was given a joyous welcome by its owner.

4/13/11 11:12 a.m. A nasty apartment neighbor is continually flipping off a man and his wife. The situation is threatening to escalate from the finger level to the verbal level.

4/17/11 10:27 a.m. A man got out of a vehicle at McNary Park and took a whole handful of dog poop bags.

4/17/11 12:02 p.m. A voice emerged from a speakerphone in a hedge on Palisades Crest Drive and threatened a man that the Russian mob was coming to get him. In the background a female was heard laughing.

4/18/11 10:29 a.m. A stepfather is upset with his 17-year-old step-daughter for constantly taking his car.

4/18/11 10:38 a.m. A shed being built on Lilly Bay Court appears to be a fort for kids. It contained BB guns and fishing poles.

4/20/11 2:03 p.m. An intruder dressed entirely in black was seen in a tree on Wax Wing Circle.

4/21/11 8:03 a.m. A 13-year-old girl is not being allowed by her grandmother to attend school because she won't clean her room.

4/22/11 12:13 p.m. A dead crow has been laying in the middle of Country Club Road for a week.

4/22/11 7:05 p.m. A mysterious vehicle with strange markings was selling ice cream to young girls on Andrews Road.

4/23/11 12:44 p.m. A duck and ducklings were reported on Kingsgate Road, but they were shooed to safety into a yard.

4/23/11 1:42 p.m. A 17-year-old daughter drove a parent's vehicle to Hillsboro and has stayed with a friend for the past three weeks. The parent does not like this and will address this issue when the daughter finally returns.

4/23/11 11:20 p.m. Police were asked to come to a home to arrest a drug seller who is emanating a demonic light.

4/27/11 8:14 a.m. A woman jogging down Canyon Drive suddenly found herself pursued by four dogs. The only response from the dogs' owner was laughter.

4/28/11 10:33 a.m. A woman performed double duty on a stroll down Kruse Way, pushing a baby in a stroller and throwing rocks at a coyote.

4/28/11 2:01 p.m. A houseguest has refused to leave his friend's couch for the past month and has badly outworn his welcome.

4/29/11 7:13 p.m. Some odd juveniles on Bandy Road are lying on manhole covers and talking into them.

4/29/11 5:57 p.m. When officers opened up the trunk of a silver Volkswagen, they found a teenager.

5/4/11 12:31 p.m. Shoes were taken off the front porch of an abode on Kerr Parkway. The thief is now wearing Puma size 13 boys shoes.

5/2/11 11:16 a.m. A driver originally thought to be drunk was actually delivering newspapers.

5/9/11 11:26 p.m. Two desperately drunk people were walking down the middle of State Street, stopping only to vomit.

5/10/11 5:19 p.m. A mama duck and a baby duck were causing problems with their antics on Brookhurst Drive and Highway 43.

5/12/11 6:07 p.m. A 15-year-old juvenile jumped out of a car and ran away. The mother is now in pursuit.

5/13/11 1:56 p.m. A woman returned to her home on Westview Drive to find the lights and TV on, but nothing was missing. Her neighbor reported the very same thing happening to her.

5/17/11 10:02 a.m. A woman became infuriated when she found that her hair had been turned purple at a salon. When she went back to complain, she was kicked out.

5/19/11 8:35 a.m. A woman told an officer she becomes upset every time she walks by her neighbor's house because her dog was attacked there several years ago. The officer advised her to not go by the house.

5/20/11 7:46 a.m. A restroom Rip Van Winkle was discovered at Roehr Park overnight.

5/20/11 11:56 a.m. Three aimless, disheveled males were thought to be up to no good as they meandered down Edenberry Drive.

5/23/11 5:48 a.m. It is feared a gaggle of baby ducks have fallen into a roadway grate on Country Club Road.

5/28/11 10:28 a.m. A border collie escaped from doggie daycare and is believed to be headed toward Millennium Park to play.

5/24/11 2:18 p.m. A million dollar prize was revealed to a man over the phone. He sincerely doubts this is authentic.

6/3/11 1:28 p.m. A son purchased video games by using his father's credit card without permission.

6/3/11 9:04 p.m. A drunk and obnoxious guy was playing guitar in front of an apartment on First Street.

6/3/11 9:07 p.m. About 20 guests were drinking beer at the back side of a location on Meadows Road. With each beer, they grew progressively louder.

6/3/11 11:17 p.m. Some high school students were overcome with laughter after driving a car into a curb on Overlook Drive.

6/4/11 9:04 p.m. A man thought to be bleeding had actually spilled ravioli all over himself.

6/6/11 2:58 p.m. A mama duck and her little duckies kept waddling onto Highway 43. An officer shooed them into some bushes.

6/6/11 3:05 p.m. A mother returned home to find that somebody had been fiddling with her car. Her children denied culpability.

6/7/11 3:21 p.m. Five teens carried a kayak through a woman's yard on Bryant Road, heading toward the Kelok Canal.

6/10/11 10:39 p.m. A son was repulsed when his mother came home with two friends who had been drinking and smoking.

6/8/11 11:03 a.m. A drunk relieved himself on a Mercedes parked at the dog park on Stafford Road.

6/9/11 12:44 p.m. Two baby ducks fell down a drain on Hopkins Lane, but an officer rescued them and returned them to the welcoming wings of their mama duck.

6/12/11 4:23 p.m. A hungry, young woman went to a residence on Ridgeway Road and asked for a bite to eat. She is also looking for a place to stay for the summer.

6/13/11 11:46 p.m. A loud group of juveniles on Melrose Street were making a lot noise while pretending to sell lemonade.

6/14/11 11:48 a.m. A purse snatcher tried to grab a woman's purse as she stood at the corner of North Shore Road and South State Street. The multitasking thief also tried to grab another person's food.

6/17/11 12:16 a.m. An apparent trail of blood leading up the stairs of a house on Edenberry Drive turned out to have been caused by a dog who had gotten into red paint.

6/17/11 6:37 p.m. A mysterious, potbellied man was seen lurking around vehicles on First Street. The man was bald and had a fireman's mustache.

6/18/11 7:30 p.m. A baby duckling fell down a storm drain near a carwash on North State Street, but it was rescued by an alert and kindly officer.

6/20/11 9:34 a.m. A tree is slowly falling on Pebble Beach Court, and at least one resident finds it becoming like the Sword of Damocles.

6/20/11 4:05 p.m. Nothing but a hound dog was howling and standing in the road on Ninth Street.

6/21/11 8:08 a.m. The dangers of dog excrement are being experienced on Evergreen Road, where numerous piles were found on the grassy right of way.

6/21/11 1:46 a.m. A man wearing a pink negligee was flashing people at an upscale hotel.

6/21/11 2:49 p.m. What was feared to be a house burglary by a gang of squatters turned out to be people doing estimate work for a real estate company.

6/21/11 6:45 p.m. A 16-year-old driver is tailgating and flipping off drivers in a crude cruise down Country Club Road.

6/22/11 1:49 p.m. Twelve goats escaped from their pen and trotted down Highway 43. However, officers helped round up the horny rascals and returned them to their corral.

6/22/11 9:21 p.m. A bag tagged "Dead Raccoon" was found in an alley on Second Street. Sure enough, there was a dead raccoon in the bag.

6/22/11 6:23 p.m. A strong chemical smell was coming from inside a convenience store where the employee was acting silly. It turned out the chemical smell is nothing unusual and the employee is always silly.

6/27/11 12:45 p.m. In a possible case of boat rage, a fat, bald man stuck out his tongue at a man and woman in another boat.

7/3/11 7:33 p.m. Three suspicious suspects wearing farm clothes are feared to be planning to steal garden tools on Country Club Road.

7/5/11 10:37 p.m. Four teenagers got out of a vehicle on Kilchurn Avenue and were slamming their bodies against houses. Kicks just keep getting harder to find.

7/6/11 9:14 p.m. In an incomplete 911 call, two subjects were overheard discussing baseball.

7/10/11 2:44 p.m. An aggressive man entered an apartment on Quarry Road and started yelling and promised to lick anyone in the house.

7/12/11 8:40 a.m. The word "butt" was written in red paint on a retaining wall on Tolkien Lane.

7/12/11 5:02 p.m. A dog was threatened with rocks by a man who claimed the dog was doing unwarranted urinating on Pioneer Court.

7/20/11 10:09 p.m. A woman saw mysterious eyes peering out at her from a bush on Hallinan Circle.

7/22/11 11:50 a.m. A disgusting concoction of ingredients were spread over two cars on Pfeifer Drive – ketchup, relish, chocolate syrup and powdered sugar.

7/24/11 10:05 p.m. A birthday party for a 5-year-old grew so loud that neighbors complained. The parents promised to quiet things down and send the children to bed.

8/3/11 9:04 a.m. A customer entered Flying Elephant deli and became so enraged by one of the paintings on display that she started yelling at employees and customers. In fact, her animus toward the picture was so great that she threatened to come back and destroy it.

8/6/11 8:15 p.m. A mother would like to know her legal rights in regard to her 25-year-old son always using her car.

8/6/11 11:26 p.m. A man told police that a woman getting very drunk and screaming was nothing out of the ordinary.

8/7/11 7:58 p.m. A case of a reckless driver doing cookies in a church parking lot turned out to be a mother teaching her daughter how to drive a car with a clutch.

8/8/11 1:14 p.m. A mother is distraught about her son constantly bringing home his crummy friend.

8/10/11 12:09 p.m. A customer at a pet supply store became irate when her purchase was placed in plastic bags, not boxed as she requested.

8/10/11 9:39 p.m. Several juveniles were contacted about trespassing on the golf course, but they said they were only looking at the stars.

8/11/11 4:13 p.m. A son is getting high, staying out late and being disrespectful.

8/11/11 4:54 p.m. A woman calling 911 for spiritual support is upset because she cannot get through.

8/17/11 2:39 p.m. A strange raccoon has been entering a woman's house, stalking her cat, opening her refrigerator and drinking milk.

8/18/11 10:57 a.m. The words "Cute Face" were written in yellow spray paint on a brick wall at Bay Creek Drive.

8/19/11 2:06 a.m. A naked man was observed walking on Boones Ferry near New Seasons. He is being considered a suspicious person.

8/22/11 1:30 p.m. A man is feeling trepidation after receiving a letter filled with Biblical admonitions about death, being rich and living off the misery of others.

8/26/11 12:52 p.m. After responding to a woman's report about smelling meth on Carman Drive and Wilmot Way, police determined that the smell actually was that of a skunk.

9/1/11 4:52 p.m. A woman found it hard to get out of her driveway due to a dead squirrel on Kingsgate Road.

9/4/11 5:53 p.m. Two runaway juveniles were found having dinner at McDonald's on Highway 43.

9/7/11 11:32 a.m. A man painted up like a clown aroused a woman's suspicion when he dropped to the ground on State Street after he spotted her watching him.

9/7/11 6:59 p.m. Some keys, a pizza and also a baby were locked inside a car parked on Westlake Drive.

9/15/11 3:31 p.m. A female client threatened a veterinarian with harm if her dog was not better by Friday.

9/19/11 2:36 p.m. Black flies are plaguing an apartment on Parkview Drive.

9/21/11 3:33 p.m. Lurkers were spotted at a yard on Black Forest Court. They are pretending to do yard work, but their total lack of tools makes this hard to believe.

9/22/11 8:58 p.m. Strange sounds, like flying saucers taking off and landing, were heard on Hallinan and Laurel streets.

9/24/11 4:02 p.m. A pilfering pooch keeps running in and out of Safeway and grabbing food.

9/24/11 6:10 p.m. A rabid squirrel is chasing people at the junior high.

9/24/11 11:34 p.m. A 15-year-old girl had some fun, fun, fun when she drove off in the blue Mercedes owned by her mother's boyfriend.

9/25/11 3:59 p.m. A verbal bout between a mother and daughter dragged on from a grocery store to a gas station.

9/25/11 6:22 p.m. An ex-husband testified that he saw his ex-wife giving marijuana to their son. However, the substance turned out to be catnip.

9/28/11 6:24 p.m. A cat stayed around a porch on Kerr Parkway for so long that this excellent description was obtained: black, long hair, bushy tail, skinny, a zip tie around its neck and meowing for more than an hour. The little rascal ran off as soon as an officer arrived.

10/1/11 8:50 p.m. Flying bologna struck a car going down Boones Ferry Road.

9/30/11 10:54 a.m. A woman became apprehensive when a swarthy man of average size came up to her and offered to fix her car for $500, then whittling the price down to $250. The man was said to have the gift of gab.

10/12/11 10:19 a.m. The appearance of a mysterious stranger at a residence on Canal Circle turned out to be the unexpected visit from a son.

10/19/11 1:43 p.m. A baby squirrel was rescued by an officer after it was injured in a driveway on Woodsman Court. The tiny creature was transported to the Audubon Society in Portland.

10/23/11 11:58 a.m. A strange instance of mischief occurred when 275 plastic forks were found stuck in the ground of a property on Camden Lane.

10/24/11 10:30 p.m. A man with a reputation for violence was heard yelling and screaming inside his residence. He was found playing video games.

11/3/11 10:47 a.m. An unconscious woman woke up to find that her head had been shaved by her landlord, whom she shares the house with. The woman claims the landlord is a Wiccan and is trying to destroy her because she is a Christian.

11/6/11 10:06 a.m. A woman's house was robbed by aliens who got away in a spaceship. Or, so she says.

11/4/11 6:08 p.m. A man came home to his residence on West Sunset Drive and found that his bed had been stolen.

11/10/11 8:43 a.m. A mother was upset after her son sneaked in someone to sleep overnight at their residence on Ash Street.

11/13/11 1:55 a.m. A maid has been barricading herself inside a man's room every night for the last year.

11/17/11 10:40 a.m. A 7-year-old woke up and was unable to find his mother. Fortunately, she was in the TV room.

11/20/11 9:12 p.m. While leaving a note chastising someone for parking in a handicapped space, a woman broke a windshield wiper.

12/1/11 8:36 p.m. The sound of moaning turned out not to be from a physical altercation but from three females who had been drinking heavily.

12/3/11 5:57 p.m. When a woman and a neighbor tried to chase away a coyote, it ran into a doggie door at a vacant house. It is believed the coyote might be living there.

12/4/11 10:45 a.m. A deadbeat guest associated with Occupy Portland has been occupying a residence for three weeks on Lakeview Boulevard.

12/5/11 6:13 p.m. A 10-year-old son ran away because he was upset his father would not allow him to go to basketball practice. Fortunately, the mother located the basketball-loving boy.

12/6/11 2:54 p.m. A man's butt was threatened with kicking in a road rage incident on Independence Avenue.

12/10/11 9:23 p.m. An extremely drunken woman was discovered down in a ditch on McNary Parkway. She claimed she was looking for Christmas decorations she had dropped.

12/27/11 3:38 p.m. A husband was worried when he called his wife at their home on Brookhurst Court and heard pounding noises in the background. It was determined that the cat had knocked a dog bone onto the floor.

12/28/11 2:72 a.m. A case of walking while intoxicated occurred on Boones Ferry when an obviously stewed individual was hitting signs with a baseball bat.

12/28/11 10:46 a.m. The lender of some money was not satisfied with the amount he was repaid and informed the borrower he had "his own way of handling this."

12/29/11 12:27 p.m. A mysterious Chihuahua was tied up in front of Lake Oswego Ice Creamery.

12/29/11 9:26 a.m. A road rage incident erupted when a car doubled-parked on Mercantile Drive.

2012

1/2/12 2:05 p.m. Four men went into a poker room on Bangy Road and started acting "weird."

1/13/12 10:53 a.m. Suspicious footprints near a residence on Palisades Terrace Drive are now believed to be those of a cleaning lady.

1/16/12 8:34 a.m. An 11-year-old called the police on his mother after she took away his PS3 game until he practiced piano. The boy was advised his mom was within her rights to do this.

1/19/12 3:39 p.m. A dog was reported to be barking for hours on Lindsay Court. However, as always happens in such cases, the dog was silent when police came to investigate.

1/20/12 3:40 p.m. Somebody spilled their Viagra on the floor of Blockbuster Video on Boones Ferry Road.

1/20/12 9:55 a.m. A woman was displeased by a car with a loud muffler that was driven onto her property on South Shore Boulevard.

1/21/12 10:58 a.m. A car was parked with such utter carelessness that it blocked four spaces in the alley behind Gemini Pub.

1/25/12 5:15 p.m. A woman's dog is being allowed to wander in protected wetlands and harass ducks.

1/26/12 11:04 a.m. A big yellow lab named "Boomer" keeps coming into Safeway and helping himself to merchandise. This resulted in his owner being cited for allowing Boomer to roam at large and also for not having a dog license.

2/1/12 5:32 p.m. A man pulled out his guitar in front of a liquor store, began playing and started to ask passers-by for contributions to his musical career.

2/1/12 10:46 p.m. A boyfriend won't stop ringing his girlfriend's doorbell.

2/3/13 3:45 p.m. A group of eight juveniles was skateboarding around Foothills Road. However, they were all wearing safety gear and their activity is legal in that area.

2/4/12 3:42 p.m. A skunk thought to be dead is still very much alive despite being hit on McVey Avenue.

2/6/12 7:26 a.m. Vehicles were struggling to get around a raccoon that was clinging to life after being hit by a car on Highway 43.

2/6/12 10:07 p.m. A too-loud washing machine is disturbing residents of an apartment complex.

2/7/12 1:04 p.m. A jogger kept running around her car because she did not know how to shut it off.

2/8/12 12:20 p.m. A man and woman have been yelling at each other for two hours. Their neighbors on Mt. Jefferson Terrace wish they would stop.

2/8/12 4:53 p.m. A report on juveniles playing soccer in a construction area on Ridgecrest Drive turned out to be erroneous. It was found that it was the construction workers who were playing soccer.

2/9/12 12:59 p.m. A possible "Gypsy" cab was driving at a high rate of speed in the North Shore Road-South State Street area.

2/9/12 3:56 p.m. A neighbor refuses to control his poodle on walks down Crest Drive, allowing the dog to go into people's yards for unspecified activity.

2/10/12 4:54 p.m. A cat under a shed on Old Gate Road evaded police efforts to catch it.

2/11/12 11:17 p.m. Horn honkers were bothering residents on Diane Drive.

2/12/12 6:04 a.m. A man was suspicious about the manner in which his morning paper was delivered.

2/13/12 8:24 a.m. The sound of what seemed to be furniture being thrown around a room disturbed residents on Jefferson Parkway. However, it turned out to be a dog playing with a ball inside.

2/15/12 2:47 p.m. A resident of Ninth Street is getting sick of a large truck parking by his property on a regular basis.

2/15/12 3:25 p.m. Two misbehaving students ditched their behavioral class at an elementary school.

2/16/12 5:08 p.m. A pair of dogs, a husky and a shepherd mix, are defying efforts to catch them on Green Tree Road and Westview Drive.

2/17/12 7:19 a.m. An apartment resident was jumping up and down on the floor to the beat of loud rock music.

2/21/12 10:39 a.m. Solicitors on Del Prado are being quite persistent in their offers to clean roofs.

2/22/12 3:34 a.m. Two subjects were deemed to be odd and out of place on A Avenue. They were delivering newspapers.

2/28/12 11:18 p.m. A thin, middle-age man dressed entirely in black was walking in a disoriented manner toward Cervantes.

3/5/12 6:18 p.m. The hose at a dog park on Stafford Road where dogs are rinsed off won't turn off. Dogs are being over-rinsed.

3/7/12 8:23 a.m. Parents are not staying in line while dropping their children off at Oak Creek School.

3/7/12 12:15 p.m. The presence of toothpaste on a counter makes it seem that someone stayed overnight at a residence.

3/15/12 8:51 p.m. A solicitor keeps knocking on doors on Sherwood Court for extended periods of time even when people refuse to come to their doors.

3/17/12 5:04 p.m. A person repeatedly trying to contact a woman who resides on Jefferson Parkway turned out to be a process server trying to deliver her a civil summons.

3/22/12 9 a.m. A 19 ½-year-old son does not want to go on a family vacation.

3/23/12 1:24 p.m. A UPS man with a big moustache was mistaken for an intruder on Glen Eagles Road.

3/27/12 9:41 a.m. Extra traffic enforcement was requested for the traffic jam at the Starbucks drive-thru window on Boones Ferry Road.

3/28/12 1:54 p.m. Unwanted phonebooks are piling up at a home on Kruse Way Place.

3/29/12 9:57 a.m. An unfriendly lady neighbor has been throwing vegetables from her deck into a man's yard on Hillside Lane. There have been ongoing problems between the woman and the man.

4/1/12 9:53 a.m. After going through garbage cans and unethically using a restroom, a man was trespassed from a restaurant on Mercantile Drive.

4/1/12 4:26 p.m. A drunken roommate is starting to make a woman feel threatened. She overheard the roommate saying "I'm going to kill her" over the phone.

4/2/12 12:02 p.m. A tempestuous teen tossed a tangerine at a man up on a ladder cleaning gutters on Oak Street.

4/2/12 4:56 p.m. A woman has constantly been chasing peacocks around the yards of her neighbors.

4/4/12 12:16 p.m. In a case of neighbor noise on Evergreen Road, one neighbor complained that a neighbor uses a leaf blower and that another neighbor constantly uses foul language.

4/6/12 9:36 p.m. A resident of Lake Grove Avenue was surprised to look out in his yard and see a stranger exercising.

4/10/12 12:22 p.m. A neighbor lady is worried that the Great Dane next door is being held in too small of a kennel.

4/11/12 6:25 p.m. Mysterious downstairs noises turned out to be four cats that were making their home there.

4/16/12 1:25 p.m. A man keeps calling a burger joint to complain about the quality of the food and service.

4/18/12 3:52 p.m. Two adult geese and five baby geese were waddling through traffic on Lakeview Boulevard in an apparent attempt to reach Oswego Lake.

4/18/12 10:30 p.m. Three skateboarders hanging around a medical office on Mercantile Drive were making people nervous.

4/22/12 5:59 p.m. In a loud incident on Kingsgate Road, a mother yelled at a woman who had yelled at her kids. The woman who had originally yelled now feels threatened.

4/30/12 3:27 p.m. A repairman tore apart an air conditioning unit on Auburn Court, but it turned out he had the wrong address.

5/3/12 9:54 a.m. Solicitors selling security systems are reportedly asking strange questions on Fernbrook Circle.

5/8/12 11:08 a.m. An upstairs neighbor is becoming increasingly noisy on Greenridge Drive.

5/9/12 8:23 a.m. A German shepherd puppy ran after a woman and pulled her skirt on Sunset Drive.

Chicken lovers team up to save feathered threesome

January 27, 2014

One of the most unlikely places to find three roosters standing around in Lake Oswego would be Lake View Village. Hundreds of people encountered the chickens on their way to drink coffee, get

The three lost roosters showed great togetherness during their sojourn in Lake View Village. Only an occasional dog could break up this chicken pack. SUBMITTED PHOTO: ELAINE TAN

yogurt or dine at a restaurant, and their reaction was invariably surprise, delight and, often, pulling out a phone camera to take a picture of this unusual event.

Longtime Lake Oswego resident Dave Schramm was grabbing a cup of coffee at Peet's when he spied the feathered trio.

"They were walking around as if they were saying, 'As long as you people leave us alone we'll let you stay,'" Schramm said.

And passersby always asked, "Where did they come from?"

There was no answer. This may always remain the Mystery of the Three Roosters. They were large, especially one big boy, rather dirty with untrimmed feathers on their feet and they really hung together, moving a few yards only when dogs tried to sniff them.

The bigger mystery was, "What would become of them?"

Thanks to Elaine Tan, who happened to be in the area getting a cup of coffee, this was a chicken story with a happy ending. She stuck with the roosters from the moment she saw them at 10:30 a.m. until they were shooed into a cardboard box and taken for boarding at the home of a bird lover. Tan made sure the birds didn't go out into traffic, fed them with donated bread from St. Honoré Bakery and made sure that dogs did not get too close. Tan was out there nearly five hours, but she didn't budge until she knew the chickens would be OK.

"I don't love chickens," Tan said. "I love animals."

While assuring the safety of the roosters, Tan used her cellphone to try to get help from some obvious sources like the police and the Portland Audubon Society. No luck. The dozens of people passing by only stopped, gaped, laughed, took photos and moved on. She did get some coffee delivered while on her vigil by "three sweet, little boys."

But Tan's tenacity finally paid off. Around 3 o'clock some true helpers showed up. Jackie Clee, who had fond childhood memories of her pet chicken, and Nicole Hsiao, who said, "I was shopping until I saw these beautiful chickens," then got a big cardboard box to put them in. As the rooster-rescue operation shaped up, other chicken-minded people drifted along until a pretty good evacuation plan fell into place. They would somehow get the roosters into the big box and load them up in Clee's car.

The sticking point was, "How do you get three chickens into a box?" There was not a chicken grabber in the bunch, but someone came up with the idea of using blankets to funnel them into the box. The action (and humorous) high point came when people running around with blankets tried to corral the birds, but the roosters easily kept shooting between gaps in the blankets.

Fortunately, a hero showed up. Mardic Price of West Linn came out of Peet's Coffee and noticed the chickens and the crowd, and as a person who was raised on a farm she knew exactly what to do: "You got to get them by the tail feathers and pick them up." The roosters squawked loudly when Price went to work, but in a few seconds the three birds were in the box.

Joy surged through the crowd, and Price's praises were loudly sung by Kellee Beaudry, who shouted, "You are awesome! You are a chicken wrangler! My god, that was impressive!"

The birds spent a pleasant night and day with the Clee family and soon found a home sweet home with Clee's bird-loving farmer friend in Canby.

"She offered to give the roosters a good home on her farm, and my husband and sons drove them out on Sunday morning," Clee said. "It looks like a great place for them, and they'll live happily ever after with the ducks and many other chickens."

Happily ever after. You can't ask for more than that.

5/10/12 10:58 p.m. A mother is objecting to her son using marijuana.

5/11/12 2:01 p.m. Dog defecation is victimizing a resident of Maple Circle.

5/11/12 9:06 p.m. After waiting for a bus for two hours, a man gave up and simply lay down on a sidewalk on Kruse Way.

5/11/12 11:02 p.m. An overenthusiastic video game club started yelling, screaming and throwing things across Overlook Drive.

5/12/12 2:10 a.m. A scary mother frightened some prowlers on West Sunset Drive.

5/12/12 8:02 p.m. Neighbors are clashing over the misbehavior of a dog on Oakridge Road.

5/15/12 4:33 p.m. Officers were not able to locate a mallard duck to take it back to Oswego Lake. A woman with Project Pooch on Third Street had given the duck a dog cookie and some water and was hoping the duck could be restored to its proper setting.

5/21/12 12:34 p.m. A boyfriend became upset after his gullible girlfriend allowed two loud-mouthed magazine salesmen to come into their apartment on McVey Avenue.

5/17/12 11 a.m. A 50-year-old woman dressed entirely in black urinated in a yard on Hastings Drive, then hastily departed from the scene.

5/23/12 6:22 p.m. A cat accidentally dialed 911.

5/24/12 7:19 a.m. An estranged wife thinks her husband might be spying on her when she shops at New Seasons.

5/25/12 2 p.m. A man was stunned when he opened a plastic bag at a dumpster in Tryon Cove and found a dead goose.

5/25/12 9:10 p.m. A naked woman was reportedly walking by the window of her house and could be easily seen by observers. Her husband said he was not sure if she was doing this intentionally or was walking back from the shower.

5/26/12 3:47 p.m. A solicitor for Comcast is being harassed by a tan man dressed entirely in green.

5/27/12 7:22 p.m. Police were invited to mediate a loud dispute between a 10-year-old and a mother.

5/28/12 12:28 p.m. A girlfriend was locked out of her home by her boyfriend, who gave the argument: "Possession is nine-tenths of the law."

5/29/12 2:29 p.m. A resident on Fielding Road is refusing to clean up the mess he made in his neighbor's yard after using a power washer. The refusal was accompanied by swearing.

6/1/12 9:53 a.m. Suspicious people in an old, battered Buick-type of vehicle were cruising down Country Club Road and feared to be casing Eighth Street for future illegal activities.

6/5/12 11:30 a.m. A large, dead fish was discovered in Millennium Plaza Park.

6/5/12 4:12 p.m. A male teen started his summer vacation by standing on the corner of Boones Ferry Road and Bryant Road and flipping off motorists.

6/6/12 10:06 a.m. An indignant husband is objecting to a neighbor taking photos of his wife as she exercises in the driveway.

6/6/12 10:35 a.m. A fervent believer was handing out religious pamphlets at Lake Oswego Junior High School in a hazardous, unsafe manner.

6/7/12 7:22 p.m. Several Chinese lanterns have shown up in a yard on Glen Haven Road.

6/11/12 6:28 p.m. A juvenile thought to be smoking something while inside a car parked at West Waluga Park turned out to just be a kid doing his homework.

6/12/12 12:38 p.m. A flaming bag of feces was left at the doorstep of a home on Hidalgo Street. Police are seeking a suspect and a motive.

6/16/12 9:27 a.m. Concern broke out on Country Club Road and Iron Mountain Boulevard when a turtle was spotted at large. It was believed to be heading toward some railroad tracks.

6/16/12 9:55 a.m. A strange man was jumping up and down at Waluga Park.

6/18/12 2:57 p.m. A politician campaigning on Walking Woods Drive told a woman he wanted her vote, although he had no material to give her.

6/19/12 8:30 p.m. An argument about potato chips broke out between a man and wife as they were watching TV.

6/19/12 11:10 p.m. Suspicion was raised on Nansen Summit when a young man came to a residence and asked for jumper cables.

6/22/12 8:55 a.m. Pink chalk was used to write on the Bank of America on Bryant Road.

6/24/12 2:45 a.m. A daughter threw an early morning tantrum when she was denied the use of her phone.

6/26/12 11:07a.m. An animal lover requested that the police stop traffic on Country Club Road to allow two deer to cross.

6/26/12 7:42 p.m. Two heavyset, middle-age women were passing a bottle in a bag between them on Reese Road and Upper Drive.

6/27/12 10:56 a.m. A daughter's ex-boyfriend stays in touch with her family by making obnoxious phone calls.

6/27/12 9:37 p.m. A scary neighbor is frightening children by coming over to tell them wild tales of spirits and demons.

6/29/12 8:21 a.m. Horses and a buggy were tying up traffic on Independence Avenue.

7/2/12 8:02 p.m. A mother is worried because her 53-year-old son has not come home yet.

7/2/12 12:35 a.m. While in her washroom after midnight, a woman became worried by some strange noises. However, she discovered they were coming from her clothes dryer.

7/4/12 1:36 a.m. Some mean people on Greenridge Drive are turning on their appliances to bother a woman.

7/13/12 8 a.m. Some melted chocolate ice cream was formed into the shape of a swastika at Sundeleaf Park.

7/17/12 12:28 p.m. When a man staggered badly coming out of a liquor

7/9/12 5:53 p.m. A daughter doesn't want her 91-year-old father joyriding with his 89-year-old girlfriend.

store, it was originally thought he was drunk. However, it turned out he had a really bad knee.

7/20/12 1:33 p.m. A neighbor on Oswego Summit has been watching his TV too loudly for the past year.

7/23/12 12:48 p.m. A strange man with long, dark hair approached a woman in the parking lot of New Seasons and asked her strange questions.

7/26/12 10:42 p.m. Hearty voices raised in unison were heard coming from a pub on B Avenue.

7/28/12 1:16 p.m. Condolea Drive was the site of a strange incident in which a pot was moved, two large plants were damaged and underwear was thrown into trees.

8/1/12 8:48 p.m. A female is dancing on the sidewalk, crossing the street and waving at people on B Avenue. It is suspected she is high on more than life.

8/2/12 8:25 p.m. Someone parked in a woman's reserved parking place at an apartment on Foothills Drive, and management refused to do anything about it.

8/5/12 10:08 a.m. A toilet in a women's bathroom on Melrose Street won't stop flushing.

8/6/12 11:51 a.m. A white chicken is running at large on Shireva Drive.

8/7/12 12:46 a.m. Drivers were disconcerted when a man got out to work on his car at the intersection of Bryant Road and Lakeview Boulevard.

8/8/12 9:54 a.m. An overly aggressive parent at the International Leadership Academy bared his teeth to the mother of another student and also used offensive language.

8/7/12 9:17 a.m. A female was tailgated and flipped off by a rude woman driver on Jean Way.

8/7/12 5:28 p.m. Two amateur mimes pretending to pull rope caused two vehicles to slam on their brakes on Carman Drive.

8/8/12 8:12 p.m. Two friendly adult boxers engaged in normal playful behavior were falsely reported to be fighting on Highlands Drive.

8/12/12 9:16 p.m. Rock throwing between neighbors broke out on Parkview Drive.

8/21/12 1:45 p.m. A pet parrot on Hillshire Drive won't shut up. Fortunately, it is only visiting.

8/22/12 4:12 p.m. A Great Dane who barks a lot is frightening people.

8/22/12 8:39 p.m. Overlook Drive was shaken up by the screams of many young girls. It turned out to be members of the Lakeridge varsity soccer team returning from soccer camp.

8/30/12 9:03 p.m. A customer was walking by a bank on B Avenue when he saw someone duck behind a counter inside. It turned out to be the manager.

9/2/12 2:34 p.m. A man lay down on the ground after getting fired from his landscaping job. But his ex-boss later came to give him a ride home.

9/4/12 7:06 a.m. Someone has been making noises over a school intercom for the past year and a half.

9/5/12 12:50 pm. A gutter cleaner knocked on a door, then ran away on Eighth Street.

9/11/12 9:34 p.m. No less than 10 text message threats have been directed at a woman.

9/13/12 7:47 p.m. Three subjects who seemed to be passed out in a park near Brookhurst Drive were discovered to be in passable condition.

9/15/12 3:48 p.m. A water-loving dog was observed swimming in Oswego Lake. When finished, the dog climbed the swim ladder on its own and returned to its owner.

9/17/12 4:19 p.m. A lady on Summit Drive cannot get her doorbell to stop ringing.

9/19/12 9:29 a.m. An unusual man is making a scene on Blue Heron Road by dancing around, talking to himself and throwing rocks.

9/19/12 3:54 p.m. A discussion about a woman's dog and the

Bible was overheard between three subjects sitting on a bench on Waluga Drive.

9/20/12 11:53 a.m. A rat crawled into a coffee shop and died.

9/24/12 9:12 a.m. A 15-year-old girl waxed wroth after her dad took away her laptop and iPod because she won't go to school.

9/25/12 12:39 p.m. A man received a dirty look when he parked in a handicapped zone.

9/27/12 4:21 p.m. A loud rooster is distressing the Fox Run/Timberline Drive neighborhood.

9/27/12 6:52 p.m. A solicitor informed a woman he is "selling charm and personality."

9/28/12 6:50 p.m. The smoking of an herbal product in Foothills Park drew the attention of police.

10/1/12 10:49 a.m. An elderly woman with an armful of leaves is walking around Boones Ferry Road.

10/1/12 6:19 p.m. While parked at a Shell Station on Boones Ferry Road, a female driver slapped a car window and left her palm print because she was upset that another woman driver didn't move her car quickly enough.

10/1/12 7:38 p.m. A woman who lives in an apartment on Carman Drive has been subjected to smoking and cursing by her upstairs neighbor.

10/2/12 5:33 p.m. A raccoon who is being rehabbed by a woman on Cedar Street has escaped. She says the raccoon is friendly. She would like to be notified if it is sighted.

10/3/12 2:19 p.m. A neighbor's dogs defecated on a woman's lawn on View Lake Court.

10/3/12 4:52 p.m. A solicitor began scrubbing a porch on Durham and Wilbur streets as a way to demonstrate her product. However, there was no one home at the time.

10/3/12 6:28 p.m. A man carrying peanut butter and several bags while looking at a map was regarded with suspicion on Walking Woods Drive.

10/5/12 10:24 a.m. An ill-tempered loony on a bicycle keeps running red lights and yelling profanities at people who voice objections to his activity.

10/5/12 1:46 p.m. A mother is worried about her daughter, who is nervous about her flight to Pennsylvania.

10/7/12 7:43 p.m. A possible pothead has been spooking customers at a pizza joint by peering through its windows.

10/9/12 3:53 p.m. An enraged 20-year-old son is throwing fruit around the house.

10/10/12 6:46 p.m. Extra police patrols were requested to stop an old man from allowing his poodle to relieve itself in a neighbor's yard.

10/21/12 9:41 p.m. A 15-year-old is refusing to leave his mother's bedroom.

10/26/12 4:53 p.m. Teens are playing tennis too loudly near Fern Place.

10/27/12 12:09 a.m. Yellers outside of an abode on Lower Drive were people who had been accidentally locked out and were hoping to wake a sleeping parent.

10/29/12 10:17 a.m. A black rabbit, possibly a pet, was seen hopping near the Hunt Club.

11/2/12 12:47 p.m. A woman nearly tripped over a terracotta planter she believes was deliberately placed there by a nasty neighbor on Foothills Drive.

11/4/12 10:55 a.m. A property manager told a mother that her son's life was worth less than her possessions.

11/4/12 7:12 p.m. A woman is seeking to find the owner of a mysterious pair of slippers she found in her house.

11/6/12 3:52 p.m. A driver totally lacking in road etiquette was speeding down Bangy Road and flipping off those who objected.

11/6/12 4:19 p.m. In a possible case of double insanity, a mother called the police to say her daughter was going crazy, then the daughter got on the phone to say that her mother was going crazy.

11/14/12 7:09 a.m. A resident of Nansen Summit is worried because a strange car has been parked in front of his house all night.

11/14/12 10:03 a.m. A citizen is seeking police observance after he was tailgated by somebody in a decrepit pickup truck.

11/23/12 5:50 a.m. A woman on Boca Raton Drive says someone has taken her clothes and shoes and will not give them back.

11/27/12 4:20 p.m. A solicitor for a security company showed a lack of salesmanship by angrily jerking a pamphlet from the hands of a homeowner on Cabana Lane.

11/27/12 4:46 p.m. A woman is sick of people checking on her and told a man, "I don't know how much more I can take."

11/30/12 2:04 p.m. A woman carrying a baby became enraged with a bus driver because he gave her the wrong time and now she must wait even longer for her bus to arrive.

11/30/12 3:25 p.m. A shaky man keeps spilling coffee as he comes in and out of a store on State Street.

12/3/12 4:31 p.m. A backside was threatened during a verbal fight over money and a car between friends on Greenridge Court. One friend informed the other that unless he unlocked the car door he was going to "kick his butt."

12/3/12 6:31 p.m. A resident of Rainbow Drive is suspicious of two solicitors for Save the Ocean.

12/3/12 6:39 p.m. A woman on North Shore Road was fearful that the person who has been threatening her was knocking on her front door. However, it turned out to be a painter looking for work.

12/8/12 3:06 p.m. A woman was wandering around Jefferson Parkway, singing and disturbing people, then walking out into traffic.

12/14/12 5:46 p.m. A man keeps coming to a barber shop even though he doesn't want to pay for a haircut.

12/18/12 1:37 p.m. A man in a yard on Candlewood Court refused to leave. It turned out he was the city ordinance officer investigating a tree-cutting incident.

12/19/12 3:12 p.m. A mother is apologizing for her son after he phoned somebody and started screaming and laughing.

2013

1/1/13 5:29 p.m. The knocking over of a mailbox on Amberwood Circle might be connected to a vodka bottle found in the shrubs nearby.

1/2/13 2:41 a.m. After being awakened by a funny noise during the night, a woman discovered that her hair and skin were turning blue.

1/4/13 4 p.m. A man in black was reportedly acting strangely and doing "Karate Kid" moves around George Rogers Parks.

1/5/13 12:27 p.m. A man followed the path of his missing canoe, which had been dragged down to the lake, and found it being used. However, the man who took the canoe was nice enough to help return it.

1/7/13 3:36 p.m. A disappointing haul was made by a thief who stole a suitcase full of dirty laundry from a vehicle on Rembrandt Lane.

1/7/13 9:10 p.m. A resident of Kimberly Circle locked himself in handcuffs and had to be rescued.

1/9/13 8:08 p.m. What was feared to be a violent fight between a couple turned out to be a child who wouldn't stop screaming.

1/18/13 6:58 a.m. A resident of the Peters Lane/Hopkins Lane area complained that construction workers were screaming, singing too loudly and playing loud music way too early in the morning. An investigation revealed that nothing out of the ordinary was happening.

1/18/13 2:03 p.m. Some "sketchy" kids were firing a model rocket in the park.

1/18/13 4:07 p.m. A weird guy wearing a baseball cap and carrying around a clipboard is peeking into windows on Wembley Park Road.

1/25/13 5:36 p.m. A woman who lives on Oak Street became suspicious when she discovered a wet footprint on her front porch. Upon further investigation, she discovered that the footprint was her own.

2/1/14 12:07 a.m. After being allowed to stay the night at her ex-husband's house, a woman stole his car.

2/5/13 3:56 p.m. A woman caused a big mess by throwing her McDonald's bag, including ketchup packets, into a mailbox on Boones Ferry Road. The rude suspect has a long, brown hair and a pierced nose.

2/5/13 4:23 p.m. An 80-year-old female driver ran a stop sign and nearly hit someone. It is hoped that she will take a re-test for her driver's license.

2/5/13 7:51 p.m. A 6-year-old son reportedly has gone out of control.

2/7/13 3:34 p.m. A dog left unattended has left a string of defecation deposits along Botticelli Street.

2/8/13 8:28 a.m. A resident of Hillside Lane is upsetting his neighbors by moving garbage cans from the proper location.

2/9/13 7:03 p.m. A woman is acting strangely after having a couple of drinks.

2/10/13 2:29 p.m. A llama was spotted on the roadway on Childs Road.

2/16/13 6:57 p.m. A dog who has been barking nonstop on Bryant Road is continuing his bad behavior by refusing to eat.

2/18/13 3:22 p.m. A wandering German shepherd fell asleep on Lakeview Boulevard.

2/22/13 1:10 p.m. A goose apparently suffering from an old leg injury was helped by an officer. The goose is now eating and appears healthy.

2/22/13 9:04 p.m. Pre-teens were misbehaving on Auburn and Hopkins Lanes, smoking, hugging and being loud.

3/2/13 3:32 p.m. In a case of inexcusably wild driving, a driver kept cutting off people on State Street and raced through a service station before parking at Picasso Salon. When confronted about this, the driver admitted to being late for a hair appointment.

3/10/13 9:49 p.m. After getting into a verbal fight with his parents, a 13-year-old boy was found hiding in the yard next door. He was wearing a ghillie suit.

3/11/13 12:55 p.m. A mother is suspicious that some person of low character is holding parties with alcohol and marijuana for underage kids on Carman Drive.

3/13/13 6:17 p.m. A suspicious woman emerged from a Honey Bucket on Fourth Street.

3/13/13 6:38 p.m. A woman claimed that children were trespassing on her property. The kids were waiting for a school bus.

3/14/13 11:49 a.m. A subject came into a building on Mercantile Drive and claimed to be a federal agent. He was not believed.

3/16/13 11:44 p.m. Another loud teen party broke out on Ridgeview Lane. While parents are out of town, their children and their friends make whoopee.

3/20/13 10:45 p.m. Two suspicious men wearing suits were seen entering a bank on Mercantile Drive. They were bank employees.

3/21/13 3:22 p.m. A group of five or six young females, including one with pink hair, was observed talking on Country Club Road.

3/22/13 11:50 a.m. A suspicious subject was walking in circles around First Citizens Bank talking on the phone.

3/24/13 5:55 a.m. A woman sought help from police even though she refused to give them her address.

3/24/13 4:34 p.m. A careless window washer was getting passersby wet as he washed windows on McVey Street.

3/24/13 8:07 p.m. Two girls explained they were lying on a sidewalk because they were looking for the pieces of a phone they dropped.

3/27/13 12:51 p.m. A man with missing teeth offered to uninstall things in a house on Lake Grove Avenue.

3/27/13 2:02 p.m. Numerous ducks are waddling onto Boones Ferry Road, prompting requests that the city build a fence around the pond.

3/27/13 4:59 p.m. A small girl was caught carrying a duck in a bag. A police officer determined that she and her friends just wanted to pet it.

3/28/13 1:07 p.m. A woman on Worthington Street was stunned when a man ran through her front door and out her back door. He did not pause to give her an explanation of his conduct.

3/30/13 9:33 p.m. A singing, drunken person was giving an impromptu concert in the alley between Our Lady of the Lake Parish and Lake Realty.

4/3/13 2:11 p.m. Upstairs neighbors are walking too loudly in their apartment.

4/5/13 5:53 p.m. A strange man keeps coming into a salon and staring at customers. This makes them uncomfortable.

4/13/13 12:29 p.m. A child called 911 because it did not want to take a nap.

4/17/13 8:56 a.m. A woman mourning a dead squirrel killed by a golden retriever was sworn at by the dog's owner.

4/23/13 1:16 p.m. A scruffy, bearded oddball was riding a bike and yelling on Lakeview Boulevard.

4/27/13 5:07 a.m. A son is incurring his mother's wrath because he keeps coming home after curfew.

4/27/13 1:24 p.m. When an owner was informed that his dog was aggressive, his response was laughter.

4/29/13 9:03 a.m. A neighbor came into a woman's house and carried away her laundry.

4/29/13 12:34 p.m. A mother has locked her daughter out of the house because she refuses to clean her room.

4/30/13 9:04 a.m. A family has received 20 text messages from a daughter's ex-boyfriend. They suggest he is highly upset about the breakup.

5/2/13 12:59 p.m. A resident was surprised when his neighbor's dog came in through the doggie door of his house on Glacier Lily Drive.

5/6/13 12:43 p.m. A person relentlessly ringing a doorbell on Chapin Way was at the wrong address.

5/13/13 5:43 a.m. A man had such a bad dream that police were called.

5/14/13 3:04 p.m. A careless skateboarding geek is impeding traffic on McVey Avenue and South Shore Boulevard. He is also flipping off those gazing at him with disapproval.

5/16/13 5:19 p.m. A 30-pound potbellied pig on the loose on Meadows Road is now in the custody of the Lake Oswego police.

5/16/13 10:32 p.m. A wife sought police input on how to keep her husband from bothering her.

8/23/13 4:59 p.m. Two people were reportedly making rhythmic movements in a restaurant bathroom on Boones Ferry Road.

5/24/13 8:52 a.m. Traffic on Boones Ferry and Country Club roads was disrupted by jaywalking ducks.

5/27/13 3:06 p.m. A man in black was singing gibberish as he strolled down an alley on A Avenue.

6/2/13 9:01 p.m. A boy with anger management problems became terribly upset when not allowed to watch what he wanted on TV. Peace was restore.

6/6/13 7:36 a.m. What was at first thought to be a snack bar burglar at Old Waluga Park turned out to be the sound of an ice maker on its last legs.

5/28/13 9:05 p.m. Neighbors and police rushed to a home where a child was heard yelling at his mother to leave him alone. It turned out the boy refused to clean his room. The mother was given options.

6/8/13 5:32 p.m. A dog broke loose and ran over a small child at George Rogers Park. The dog owner sought to find the child's parents and apologize.

6/9/13 12:15 a.m. A woman was suspected of DUII after her unsteady driving on Stafford Road. It turned out she had just gotten new glasses and was having trouble getting used to them.

6/11/13 1:04 p.m. A woman who keeps coming up with weird ideas is starting to worry her sister.

6/11/13 2:18 p.m. A brother keeps breaking items and then calling his sister to say, "Excuse me, ma'am," over and over.

6/13/13 6:50 p.m. A woman objected to having her head shaved by an acquaintance.

6/14/13 10:20 a.m. A son who was sleeping too soundly did not answer the phone when his mother kept calling.

6/18/13 11:59 a.m. A small pig left home and was running loose at Freepons Park. An officer arrived to take the errant porker back to his home on Hallinan Circle.

Police capture elusive pig after struggle

Porker's gambit ends thanks to canny officer, alert citizen

May 23, 2013

The pig file of the Lake Oswego Police Department has just added another case.

A round but elusive pink pig escaped all efforts to catch it the

This pig was having a good time rooting around until it was captured and placed behind bars after a squealing struggle. It is now safe and sound back home. SUBMITTED PHOTO: BILL ABADIE

evening of May 16 near Freepons Park until Officer John Brent of the Lake Oswego Police Department arrived and cornered the annoyed animal. The pig was extremely fast and very loud, but Brent was able to grab the squealing rascal and place it in his patrol car.

The pig was transported to the LOPD's downtown headquarters and placed in a holding cell. The next move was to contact Officer Ulli Neitch of the Milwaukie Police Department, who is widely known for her work with animals. Neitch said she was just getting into a patrol car to drive to Lake Oswego when she got the word that the pig's owner had called and had taken the pig back home.

This story had a happy ending, but for a while it was touch and go.

It started on May 16 at around 5 p.m., when Bill Abadie, a resident of Meadows Drive, came upon the pig rooting around in a yard at the corner of Meadows and Hemlock. The action began when Abadie's neighbor, Betsy Ouchida, came along walking her dog, which spotted the pig and pulled her over so he could get nose-to-nose with the animal.

"The pig was about 25 pounds and pink and white — about the size of a potbellied pig," Abadie said. "He wasn't afraid of us or the dog."

Abadie sprang into action and tried to capture the pig, but the pig would not allow him to get close. So, Abadie reported the loose pig to police. Fifteen minutes later, Brent arrived. He was the right man for the job.

"He's an expert," said LOPD Capt. Dale Jorgensen. "He is quite the animal whisperer. Whenever we have weird animal calls he seems to be on duty. He handled the case of the bald eagle caught in the tree and recently with the cougar sightings."

It was no easy task, however, for Brent to corral the pig, who was determined to keep on rooting. Abadie was fortunate enough to observe the whole incident.

"It was really funny watching him trying to grab the pig and put it in the back of the patrol car," Abadie said.

Brent kept his sense of humor during the situation, cracking pig jokes the entire time and finally got the pig in custody by pretending to have food.

Brent's fellow officers were delighted that he brought in the pig and tried to take photos of it in the patrol car. Only an hour and a half after the pig was put behind bars, the LOPD got a phone call.

"I've lost my pig," a man said.

"We were able to reunite them," said Jorgensen, who noted there was another pig-on-the-loose incident several years ago.

News that the pig was home again was greeted with relief.

"It was good to hear," Abadie said. "I'm glad it didn't end up on somebody's breakfast table."

6/19/13 9:17 a.m. A woman feared that large, muddy paw prints on her patio might be those of a cougar. However, police discovered them to be raccoon tracks.

6/20/13 3:36 p.m. A lack of brotherly love was indicated when a man stole his brother's camcorder, pressure washer and miscellaneous tools, with a total value of $1,400.

6/20/13 1:56 a.m. A woman was not surprised to get an email reporting that there was a warrant for her neighbor's arrest. He is a known heroin user and is a sloppy dresser.

6/24/13 7:25 a.m. A man is convinced that a sudden flash of light brown was a mountain lion.

6/25/13 9:30 p.m. The sound of knocking and strange voices turned out to be a malfunctioning humidifier.

6/26/13 6:02 p.m. A solicitor without a clipboard is raising suspicion on Alder Circle.

6/26/13 6:14 p.m. In a case of really bad teenage driving, a driver crossed over a double line, tailgated another car and almost hit an oncoming vehicle before parking at the high school.

6/30/13 11:18 p.m. A screen was cut at an apartment on Oakridge Road. Later, money was found left on it.

7/2/13 10:29 p.m. A man was trapped inside the restroom at Hazelia Field until an officer arrived and instructed him to press a button on the wall that would unlock the door.

7/3/13 1:35 p.m. Coyotes on a woman's lawn on Grand Oaks Drive seem to be dehydrated.

7/23/13 12:57 p.m. A mother was worried because her adult children are threatening to move back home.

7/23/13 6:35 p.m. An elderly woman thought to be in trouble was just listening to the end of a radio program before getting out of her car.

7/24/13 5:45 p.m. A search for a missing 5-year-old son ended under the child's bed.

7/29/13 12:39 p.m. A resident of Ridgeway Road is trying to disguise the porn he is watching by playing music loudly.

8/7/13 5:32 p.m. A pig broke out of its backyard and was eating apples in a backyard on Hallinan Circle. A police officer put a halt to the pig's fruit feast.

8/10/13 2:52 a.m. A man got upset about seeing a bird stuck in a cup holder in a truck. However, an officer found that it was only a toy mouse.

8/20/13 12:30 a.m. The sound of kids whispering and coughing and the odor of marijuana aroused suspicions they might be guilty of illegal shenanigans.

8/11/13 11:29 a.m. Subjects playing kickball on South Shore Boulevard agreed to stop cheering so loudly.

8/21/13 7:34 p.m. A mother has not talked to her son for a year and still doesn't want to talk to him.

8/23/13 5:06 p.m. A customer aroused suspicion with his constant trips to the bathroom. His trips turned out to be legitimate.

9/3/13 2:42 p.m. A mother is distressed because her two sons will not stop fighting.

9/5/13 6:23 p.m. While cruising the Internet, a father noticed graffiti at a location on A Avenue. He has a good idea who did it: his daughter.

9/12/13 1:20 p.m. During an argument at school, one brother threatened to harm another brother. This threat stemmed from the belief that one thought the other to be disrespectful to family members.

9/13/13 11:47 p.m. While wandering to find the source of the odor of marijuana, a man encountered a wandering skunk.

9/15/13 5:50 p.m. What seemed to be a loud, vociferous argument turned out to merely be two drunken friends walking home.

9/16/13 8:47 a.m. A coyote attacked a squirrel and a peacock on Cortez Court. It got the squirrel, but the peacock escaped.

9/17/13 8:26 a.m. A woman is denying accusations by her ex that she has mental problems, but she does want police counseling on how she can stop being such a fast driver.

9/22/13 10:56 p.m. A mother and daughter got into a screaming match over having the girl clean her room.

9/26/13 7:28 a.m. A beanie-wearing bigmouth rolled down his car window and started swearing at other drivers.

10/1/13 10:06 a.m. A man was weirdly waving his arms as he stood on a street corner. He was listening to music while waiting for the bus.

10/6/13 10:01 p.m. A mother managed to lock herself outside of her house. She was unable to rouse her 13-year-old son, who was sound asleep inside.

10/8/13 12:12 a.m. A woman called in to say that she had smoked marijuana and now felt like she was going to die. Rest was recommended.

10/15/13 6:15 p.m. Disconcertion is being caused by a loud, belligerent person who is dragging a cat around on a leash.

10/16/13 4:43 p.m. A family suspects that their landlord is trying to turn the son into the devil. Advice and options were given by police.

10/18/13 8:42 a.m. A suspicious-looking man with a beard and long nose was staring in a disconcerting fashion at a house on Uplands Drive.

10/18/13 3:03 p.m. A woman kept yelling "Help me!" until a police officer arrived to help her. She was having digestion problems.

10/23/13 8:28 p.m. A distinguished-looking man with salt-and-pepper hair, wearing a button-down shirt, slacks and shoes (all black) just hot-footed away from Stafford's restaurant after executing a dine-and-dash. Earlier he performed a similar maneuver at Oswego Grill.

10/21/13 4:52 p.m. A man has aroused suspicion on Melrose Street by darting in and out of the bushes.

10/24/13 8:12 p.m. A man stumbling along Fosberg Road was simply very tired of walking. He was given a ride home by officers.

10/25/13 12:41 p.m. An outsider keeps coming in to hang out in an employee break room. The person is described as a matronly woman wearing sunglasses.

10/29/13 11:52 a.m. A Great Dane named Shamus has run away. He should be easy to spot.

10/31/13 6:41 p.m. A skinny man in a gray sweatsuit was walking around and carrying his shoes. This was thought to be odd.

11/2/13 10:08 p.m. A man with a crowbar aroused worry in a woman. But it turned out he was actually carrying a flute.

11/5/13 2:16 a.m. A mother asked the police to help urge her son to come out of the basement.

11/5/13 11:59 a.m. While hitchhiking on Greenbrier Road, a man broke into a dance. He was found to be normal and later he caught a bus.

11/6/13 12:29 p.m. A thief who is into yard decorating stole miscellaneous plants, ceramic mushrooms, a large fern topiary, flower baskets and a white pumpkin.

11/8/13 8:51 a.m. A man wearing a plaid shirt looked dazed and out of it when he walked very slowly into a coffee shop. However, he was not as spaced out as he looked.

11/12/13 4:21 p.m. A grandmother is worried about her 17-year-old granddaughter dating a 19-year-old.

11/14/13 9:45 a.m. Two suspicious loiterers at a business turned out to be culinary students.

11/20/13 10:08 a.m. A man is going from door to door flapping his arms like wings. It is believed he is as high as a bird.

11/25/13 9:51 a.m. People at Millennium Plaza Park became scared when they saw a man with a fully exposed butcher's knife coming their way. However, the man turned out to be a chef merely going to work.

12/2/13 1:40 a.m. A man requested that police talk to him about things in his life that are bothering him.

12/2/13 2:45 p.m. After answering a knock at her door on Park Forest Avenue, a woman was confronted by a man staring at her.

12/4/13 11:01 a.m. A 14-year-old boy refuses to get out of bed and go to school. The lad was advised of the law requiring kids to go to school.

12/7/13 4:13 p.m. A man found a sleeping bag in bushes near Hidalgo. He suspects someone has been sleeping in it.

12/8/13 2:36 p.m. Because his neighbor in a condo is acting strangely, a man suspects he is holding hostages.

12/8/13 5:29 p.m. When a 16-year-old son arrived home with some marijuana, his parents snatched away his pipe and broke it.

12/16/13 5:42 p.m. A small, light-brown terrier wearing a sweater with a penguin that says "Sloppy kisses" was found in Sierra Vista Drive. A good Samaritan is holding onto the pooch with the embarrassing sweater.

2014

1/1/14 8:14 p.m. Alarming screams in a neighborhood turned out to be coming from kids happily jumping on a trampoline.

1/13/14 3 p.m. A driver kept following a woman until he finally stopped and asked if he could fix the dent in her car.

1/14/14 7:26 a.m. A 13-year-old daughter is refusing to go to school. In fact, she won't even get out of bed.

1/17/14 9:34 a.m. Three chickens were at large in front of Peet's Coffee in Lake View Village. They were not creating a hazard but they did cause a wide flutter of interest. A police officer attempted to catch the chickens but they eluded him.

1/21/14 6:44 p.m. A resident of Twin Fir Road refuses to turn off his water even though it is seeping into the house of his next-door neighbor.

1/24/14 12:59 p.m. A mother hopes a visit from a police officer will convince her son not to park in handicapped parking spots.

1/25/14 11:36 p.m. A brawl broke out between a mother and her 16-year-old daughter after the maternal figure took away the teen's cell phone.

1/30/14 3:55 a.m. A woman woke up to find that somebody had shaved her head.

1/30/14 8:34 a.m. A vehicle caused distress when it was parked more than 12 inches from the curb on E Avenue.

1/31/14 2:46 p.m. A filmmaker making a zombie movie notified police that there would be lots of screams coming from South State Street.

2/17/14 10:32 a.m. Conscientious citizens were seen chasing a horse running loose at Luscher Farm.

2/22/14 11:04 a.m. A black-and-white speckled chicken was attempting to cross South State Street. It was trying to get to the other side.

2/20/14 8:42 a.m. A middle-age man and woman got together despite restraining orders against both of them.

2/23/14 6:21 p.m. An employee of a convenience store on Boones Ferry Road was found passed out in a flower bed. He had gotten into the beer supply.

2/25/14 4:52 p.m. Some apartment neighbors got into an argument when one of the neighbors went into the other's house uninvited to check on the condition of a cat.

2/26/14 10:11 a.m. A man wearing headphones looked dazed and confused as he erratically zig-zagged on his morning walk. He explained he was warming up before his workout at Club Sport.

3/6/14 2:29 p.m. A woman claiming to be Michael Jackson's spiritual guide keeps coming into a bank, claiming she has an account. She is spooking bank employees, and her two cohorts standing outside are bugging them, too.

3/27/14 1:44 p.m. A man who got a bad haircut started yelling at the barber who did it.

4/1/14 6:50 p.m. A resident of Lee Street is finding that her "No Soliciting" sign does not work.

3/1/14 9:44 a.m. After leaving the Firehouse Pub, a man decided to take a sponge bath in the fountain across the street.

4/8/14 3:12 p.m. A stray dog ran into a woman's home on West Sunset Drive and won't come out.

4/14/14 3:15 p.m. An extortionist dog sitter has kidnapped a woman's pit bull and will not say where the dog is located. The dog sitter wants to be paid an additional $700 instead of just the $300 that was paid.

4/15/14 10:27 a.m. What appeared to be three gun shots on Country Club Road turned out to be a chemistry class at Lake Oswego High School performing experiments on combustion.

4/24/14 1:20 a.m. A man has asked police to search for his missing dog. One of the dog's traits is that he doesn't come when he is called.

4/27/14 9:04 a.m. A dog owner whose neighbor had reported his dog for barking too much insisted that his dog had only barked for 10 minutes and was a relatively quiet animal.

4/30/14 10:28 a.m. An injured squirrel suddenly jumped up and climbed a tree just as an officer showed up to check on its condition.

5/8/14 7:40 a.m. A young blonde was having fun fun fun on Overlook Drive, driving recklessly, speeding and passing on the right.

5/1/14 12:49 p.m. A restaurant owner is creating a Dickensian environment for his employees. That is, he is treating them badly.

5/13/14 6:30 p.m. A father complained that a drunken member of a college rowing team started yelling at his son at George Rogers Park because the boy tripped over a duck.

5/19/14 3:47 p.m. Two suspicious-looking teens were lagging around a house on Douglas Circle, perhaps casing it for a future criminal endeavor. They were wearing hoodies and black sweatshirts, which somewhat gave away their intentions.

5/23/14 9:53 a.m. After another driver threw a piece of trash at her car, a woman drove in hot pursuit of the trasher.

5/26/14 8:21 p.m. A woman was informed that her ex-husband had stolen things from her. The informant was his current girlfriend.

5/27/14 3:14 p.m. A worried woman on Lakeview Boulevard has spotted a coyote looking at a deer and a fawn by Oswego Lake. If necessary she will rush to the rescue of the deer with her trusty broom.

5/28/14 12:44 p.m. A stray bunny was picked up on Quarry Road. The little girl who found the bunny wants the owner to describe it before she returns the cute rabbit.

6/1/14 7:38 a.m. A woman at first thought her car had been stolen while she was drinking coffee at Chuck's Place. However, it turned out she had left the car in neutral and it had rolled downhill.

6/5/14 10:18 a.m. A dog on the loose caused a traffic tangle at the traffic circle at Borland and Stafford roads. A police officer and five public-spirited citizens tried to capture the errant pooch, but they only caused more traffic problems.

6/7/14 4:08 p.m. A woman driver called AAA to have her broken car towed, but when it was being lifted up for towing she began screaming that her car was being stolen.

6/19/14 12:58 p.m. In a cat call to a residence on Kingsgate Road, a police officer left a message for the condo owner to let the cat out or else give the police permission to enter the residence and check on the cat's condition.

6/20/14 8:56 a.m. After drinking some high-energy beverages, some boys plotted to dress up in Gillie suits and go hang out at Westlake Park.

6/21/14 5:38 p.m. A woman was disturbed when a female neighbor drove up next to her, stopped and started snapping her gum.

6/22/14 11:16 p.m. Police were given a bum steer when they were informed about a screaming female on Kerr Parkway. She was only flossing her teeth before going to bed.

6/26/14 4:22 p.m. A woman struggled to keep her bathtub from overflowing before the police showed up.

6/27/14 12:36 p.m. A resident of Kerr Parkway opened his front door and found a neighbor's dog charging at him. He could barely get his door closed before the dog could reach him. At the other end of the leash was the dog's overpowered owner.

Are you one of the many people that need a weekly dose of "No Call Too Small"?

No worries. You don't have to wait for our next book. We have several ways for you to get your weekly fix of life in Lake Oswego.

SUBSCRIBE – This is the best and only way for you to see the entire police log every week. We'll mail the entire newspaper to your home every Thursday (unless you live outside of the area and then it will depend on the postal service). A local one-year subscription is only $39 (out of area $64).

Call 503-620-9797 to subscribe or go online to lakeoswegoreview.com and click the SUBSCRIBE button located on the left rail slightly down on the page.

FACEBOOK – We also preview our weekly police log on Facebook every week. Like us on Facebook at facebook.com/LakeOswegoReview

TWITTER – Follow us on Twitter at @LOReview